Total Tripping

Asia

CARL LAHSER

Order this book online at www.trafford.com
or email orders@trafford.com

Most Trafford titles are also available at major online book retailers.

Printed in the United States of America.

ISBN: 978-1-4907-4454-4 (sc)
ISBN: 978-1-4907-4455-1 (e)

Trafford rev. 08/26/2014

 www.trafford.com

North America & international
toll-free: 1 888 232 4444 (USA & Canada)
fax: 812 355 4082

Contents

Osan, Korea

1979

In 1979 I was working as an environmental engineer for the Navy on Guam. My wife and I had sent our son to spend the summer with his cousins at my brother's house in San Antonio, Texas. I heard about an R&R flight from Andersen AFB on Guam to Osan Air Base near Seŏul in South Korea. Since our son was still out of the house, we decided to go. We would leave on Thursday morning and return Sunday morning on an Air Force KC-135 aerial tanker.

We packed light but took heavy jackets since the plane would be doing training refueling along the way and would be depressurized and without heat in the cabin. We drove up to Andersen on the north end of the island before daylight and left the car with some friends on base. They drove us to flight operations where we signed in and waited for the plane to load. There were ten others waiting for the plane. We paid for box lunches and were ready to go. There were about twenty passenger seats in the front half of the plane. After we were seated we were briefed on the flight and safety regulations. The engines roared to life and we away we went.

The ride was tolerable for about two hours as we flew north towards southern Japan. Then the plane was depressurized for the first refueling operation. I went back to watch over the boom operator's shoulder. A pair of F4 Phantoms was flying in formation close below and behind us. One of the Phantoms crept up on us as the boomer talked him into position to hook up on the nozzle on the end of a long boom. He clicked into position and the boomer delivered a token load of 500 pounds of jet fuel. The Phantom disconnected and backed off disappearing into the night. The second Phantom followed the same procedure. A few minutes later the same two planes repeated this practice maneuver. About a half hour later another flight of phantoms appeared and went through the same procedure.

We flew north across the western Pacific Ocean into the East China Sea north of Okinawa. We turned to the northwest and flew west of Kyūshū then through the Korea Strait and across Korea to Osan about sunrise. We off loaded near base operations and were told to be back early Sunday morning for the return flight. Base transportation took all of us and dropped us at the Osan Hotel in downtown Osan. We passed the large camouflaged concrete block house and the machine gun pits guarding the main gate along the way.

The room at the hotel was about 10X12 feet or 3X4 meters. I asked for a full size bed and got a single bed. This was the Korean equivalent:

for instance a king size bed is a double queen. This resulted on lots of mistakes in buying brass beds and the sheets and quilts to fit them. The bath was tiny but Western style. We were on the fourth floor overlooking houses and gardens and across town. It was interesting to see the neighbors start the day peeing on the beans in the garden. This was a city planner's nightmare with homes, businesses, high rise hotels, garden plots, live stock intermingled.

I looked at the construction of a new building across from the hotel. It was to be four stories with concrete block walls and a concrete slab floor. First thing to notice was the use of bamboo for the scaffolding tied together with some kind of twine. Through the scaffolding ran a switchback of 2X10 planks that served as a path for wheelbarrows of concrete and other materials being delivered to the upper floors. I did not see any steel reinforcing rods and was curious as to how the floor would be poured a couple cubic feet at a time. In Hong Kong a few years later they were still using bamboo scaffolds for buildings up to 20 floors, but had safety nets hung every four floors. Roof mounted cranes replaced the wheel borrows and delivered large buckets of concrete.

The hotel manager took my wife and I and a couple of other guests out for a Korean dinner. We traversed several alley sized streets to his *hanok* or house. In the dining room everyone sat on the floor around a brazier that cooked *kalbi* – thin marinated sliced beef served with "Korean sauce". There was also *kimchi* and *japchae* and roasted garlic pods served with a spicy sauce. Ob beer was available during the meal but they found a Coke for my wife. Following the meal we were served hot tea with roasted soy beans and fresh fruit. I thought everything was good and consumed a quantity of the roasted garlic pods. The next morning my wife complained that my dragon breathe could peel the wall paper.

Kimchi or *kimchee* is the national dish of Korea. It is made by brining and fermenting cabbage, radish, ginger, cucumber and, since the 1590's, chili peppers with shrimp or fish sauce. It has a strong persistent odor that caused many US troops returning from the Korean War to burn their uniforms. Korea spent millions on research to sterilize and deodorize kimchi so it could be taken to outer space for the first Korean astronaut. *Kimchi* is both highly seasonal and regional. Summer or *yeolmu kimchi* is usually radish and cucumber. Autumn or *baechu kimchi* is mostly cabbage and salt. Winter or *kimjang kimchi* is made from a variety of vegetables and more fish and ferments longer.

On Friday we went shopping in downtown Osan and found a lot of clothing and cheap tennis shoes. We bought several pairs of tennis shoes for our son to change into as he grew. He grew so fast that in the next couple years he skipped a couple shoe sizes. .

We stopped for lunch at a Korean pizza place. I have eaten many pizzas in many places and think they served probably the worst pizza I ever had. Lots of garlic, a really spicy sauce and no meat. Heartburn city.

My wife went back to the room with heartburn while I looked around some more. Cheap sporting goods like ski jackets and running shoes. I looked closely at some of the shoes and found they were seconds or factory rejects with misaligned soles, smeared glue and other structural or cosmetic booboos. These were rejects of major brands made in Korea and sold locally. They were priced based on the severity of the defect.

I stopped in a two table tea shop for ginseng tea served with roasted soy beans and headed back to the hotel. My wife was not feeling well. She took some Tums and decided on no supper. I went out to a local hole in the wall restaurant recommended by the hotel for a big bowl of *chompong*.

The night time temperature was in the 90's and so was the humidity. Not a leaf stirred. There was a slight smell of kimchee fermenting from kimchee pots buried in the neighborhood gardens. Summer and fall kimchi fermented fast in 3-4 weeks.

We managed to survive the night on the tiny mattress. After an American breakfast in the hotel, we decided to go into Seŏul. The hotel clerk gave directions to the bus station and changed a few dollars into the local *won*. And we were off to see the world of Seŏul.

The bus route wound through the hills and along the Ob River into an increasingly urbanized area. The river was low and the river bed was what looked like chert cobbles. After the bus, we took a taxi to the *Dongdaemun* cloth market. The streets were from two narrow lanes to six or more in each direction with busses, cars, trucks, push carts, pedicabs, wheel borrows and animal drawn wagons mixing and mingling with pedestrians with loads of produce on their back.

This was one of three large cloth markets. It was about a square mile of shops selling cloth in any kind or quantity imaginable. This was surrounded by tailor shops many of them specializing in military uniforms.

We stopped for burgers then took another taxi to the *Gyeongbokgung* palace and gardens. This palace was built in 1395. Called the north palace (northern most) it is/was the largest of the five imperial palaces. It was destroyed by Japan in the 1590s and not rebuilt until 1868. The Japanese destroyed part of it in WWII and constructed the Japanese Administrative Building on the site. Much of the palace has been restored and houses the National Museum. We visited the museum and garden for a couple hours before returning to the bus station for the trip back to Osan.

We stopped at a shop selling Korean art and antiques. The owner said traditional antiques were not legal to export. He also explained that the so-called Korean antiques were classed as pre- or post-Japanese since the Japanese had removed most of the cultural items during their occupation. He did have an interesting variety of celadon and other replicas which we did not buy. I did purchase some pre-WWII primitive farm kitchen stoneware.

Sunday morning we took a taxi out to the base about sun up. We had just arrived on base when the base was closed down while a SR-71 Blackbird dropped out of the dark sky and taxied directly into one of the hangers. I thought this plane was supposed to be black but this one looked brownish.

After breakfast at the operations snack bar we sat around for a couple hours until the flight was called. Near noon, we loaded up and boogied into a clear sky. Following a couple more refueling operations along the way we landed at Andersen AFB shortly after sunset. I hitched a ride with the sky cops (base security police) to pick up our car, and we were home an hour later.

Carl Lahser

Hong Kong

1979
Carl Lahser

Contents
Hong Kong visit, 1980

Flying into Hong Kong

The interminable western Pacific night
finally punctured by a yellow speck
then more
by Macao,
Hong Kong
and the coastal island lights

The yellow glow
of low voltage and low wattage lights
differs from the stark white
or the peach colored halogen lights
of the Western world.

More lights appear as we begin
the approach to Kai Tak airport
diving into a mass of fireflies.
Diving.
Diving.
Then ships' masts begin zipping past.
just before we gently touch contested earth
I look into a living room flying past
with the TV on
two old people sitting on a sofa.
Should I say hello or excuse me?

Full Moon

A full moon and setting sun
The red and orange of sunset
contrast the pastel gold of moonrise
like chrome and pewter.

I have watched five hundred risings of the moon

> -floating over sparse spruce and aspen forests
> and cranberry bogs of the arctic;

> -surfacing from long tranquil fetches of ocean
> or leaping over waves crashing on coral reefs;

> -swinging out of steamy jungle green
> in the sudden tropical night;

> -eerily lighting the ruins of a hundred
> dead or dying civilizations;

> -moon washing maize and squash patches,
> Montane valleys and desert vistas;

> -from aircraft where rising and setting of the sun
> or the moon can be played like a yo-yo;

> -peeking through breaks in storm clouds.

The best and most exciting full moons
have been and will be
in your company.

AUTUMN MOONLIGHT

Hills
   and valleys
     in the ivory
a u t u m n
      moonlight

     An
       owl call
Beckons wandering souls

          Hills
        to ponder
      in a cool breeze

A valley   of ethereal shade
invites   exploration
Inviting   scents
    abide   in the
    autumn   air

Cast caution to the wind
and claim the wonders of the night

*****

Autumn Renku

Unfortunate man
In such a hurry that he
will drink first steeped tea
While the kettle boils and steams
time to rest, relax, reflect

Kung fu cha is strong
Made outside on open fire,
heady odor wafts
Tea jar, teapot, all I need-
art, utility, and friends

Sun sinking, sky orange
Martins sing chee cha chee chee
Water boils for us
Teahouse on a pond, frogs sing,
poems, warm fire, sounds of night

Thunder in the night
Mist swirls as morning birds wake
Hot tea and yogurt
Tai chi in the still wet grass
Sun and hours of toil until dusk

*****

Demise of the Monkey,
Night of no Moon
One One day 4649

The golden sun-orb
descends deliberately
towards a lucky red horizon
on a clear, cool evening.
No moon precedes of follows the sun
pursued by the Eastern dragon of night.

So dies the Year of the Monkey
and begins a night of no moon.

The dawn breaks red,
then orange.
the mother hen sun
with the noon under its wing
cracks the vault of heaven.

With a faint "ert, ert" of a young cock
the Year of the Rooster begins.

Auspicious signs for the new year.

*****

DIM SUM

Dim Sum means "light snack" usually
accompanied by Yum Cha or tea and talk.
At the Sam Pan Garden Dim Sum
begin with shrimp dumpling (Har Gau)
and spareribs (Pai Kwat)
and black dragon tea

steamed dumpling
    with a thousand year egg (Cha Siu Bau)
chrysanthemum buns
    with many fillings
adventurous dishes
    like steamed duck feet
steamer baskets with wondrous smells
Jasmine tea.

Glutinous congees with raw fish or taro
salted Ba-Jen congee with sea cucumbers
Indian tea

Deserts like La Ba, congee of fruit
Mi Kao, the sweet rice cakes
Ba Bao rice
fried bananas with honey or dragon eyes
Rare white tea

Dim Sum
Dim Sum
Dim Sum

*****

First Hours of Fall

Sitting beside you
on an afternoon in early fall
evoked memories
of sitting beside you
on pleasant afternoons in spring
and of missing you all summer
when you sat beside another.
What a long miserable summer it was.

Fall afternoons
brought you back.
Where will we be
when winter winds
begin to sigh?
Where will we spend our winter?

*****

Polluted night Renku

The moon on high is
a white silver disc in jet
the moon is red brass
when air pollution sting my
eyes and irritates my lungs

*****

The White Bat

Plums had set on the old gnarled tree
when a hoary white bat
found us, circled us
and gave us a thousand years.

Many plums have ripened.
Our time is held in
a polished ironwood box
carved with a peach
and bats on the four corners.
The box rests on a table
between our chairs.

Take my hand.

I will keep you as warm
as our old kung
until the owl cries in the night.

*****

Hong Kong Chestnuts, 1979

A walk down Nathan Street at dawn
with my wife and son
past Kowloon Park.
No one is in sight
except a chestnut vendor a block away
warming his hands as chestnuts begin to roast.
No one else is out in the cool white dawn.

The chestnut man eyes us warily
and greets us in English
with a Shanghai accent.
I show off, reply in Mandarin
and warm my hands.
Then I purchase a bag of hot chestnuts
and put one hot nut
in each of my son's jacket pockets.
The old man grins and wishes us well.

*****

Nathan Street II, Hong Kong, 1979

A walk down Nathan Street at dawn is a private walk
I cross Nathan Street and look in the windows at solid gold statues
Buddha, Kwan Lin, Li Po the drunken poet.

A binjo man comes out of a side street
with two large plastic jugs of urine
collected from other white plastic jugs
sitting on the sidewalk
hugging the wall connected by tubing
to second-floor living quarters.
He scurries along Nathan Street
not taking time to look at the gold.

A small jewelry store opens for the day.
The proprietor invites me in for tea.
We share his tea and my chestnuts.
I buy a cheap pair of Taiwan jade earrings for half price
Because, as first customer of the day,
I must buy something
to bring him good luck for the day.

I wish him luck and head for the Star ferry landing.

*****

THE WALK

Mid afternoon on a fine fall day
Overcast and humid after a quick shower
Footfalls muffled by damp leaves
A jay screams in the distance
An acorn falls shattering the heavy stillness
We walk not speaking
Holding hands where the path is wide enough
To a log on the edge of a clearing
Sitting and watching small birds flit
Through the changing and thinning leaves
Holding hands
Memorizing worn knuckles
And scarred fingers
Warts and bluish veins
Until we agree its time to return
Up the silent path through the half light

*****

Going to Hong Kong Central

South on Nathan Road
passing Kowloon Park
with old folks doing Tai Chi
and trimming the flowerbeds

Right on Salisbury Rd
towards the old Clock Tower,
the last reminder of
the old Kowloon-Canton Railway Station
to the Star Ferry terminal.
A green and white ferry, Twinkling Star,
has just arrived.

HK60c to join the lower deck
second class crowd
for an eight minute ride
from Tsimshatsui to
Hong Kong Island Central District.

***

Lascar Row or Cat Street, Hong Kong

Just off Hollywood Road
is Cat Street where,
shoulder to shoulder with the crowd,
we wandered the flea market fair.

My son spotted a bright red jacket
which he wanted to try on real bad.
The old woman handed him a blue one
but my son insisted on the red.

In broken English she explained
Red was the color for a girl.
She would not sell a red jacket to a boy
and allow him to be subject to ridicule.

In a world of the poor,
a principled merchant.

*****

Charles at Tiger Balm Garden

On the tour of Hong Kong Island one of our stops was Tiger Balm Garden. My wife and 8-year-old son, Charles, and I had fifteen minutes to look around this unique garden of painted concrete and plaster castles, pagodas, mythological figures, monsters and dragons and the Hew Par mansion. The three hectare garden was built by Aw Boon Haw famous for Tiger Balm salve. It is formally known as the Aw Boon Haw Garden at a cost of HK$16 million in 1935. Some call it the Chinese Disneyland.

While the tour guide was giving his talk Charles took off looking on his own. At the end of the scheduled time we looked for Charles and called his name with no answer. The tour guide was upset and wanted to leave so we stayed to find our wandering son.   I went through the whole park calling.   Some other tourist said they would help but when the heard Charles was 8, blond and blue–eyed they told my wife that they had heard of little boys being kidnapped. This upset my wife.

My wife was ready to call the police when Charles came out of hiding and hollered "Boo". He had not been ready to go in fifteen minutes so he hid and watched the panic.

We stayed in the park another half hour because he wanted to show us some real neat things he had found. A taxi took us to Food Street for lunch. We spent the afternoon looking around Causeway Bay and Wanchai.

Night way falling when we took the Star Ferry from Wanchai to Kowloon. Charles was tired and missed the city lights and harbor traffic.

*****

Walk Through a Street Market

Along a sidewalk and alley stalls

Baskets with crabs tied with grass
fresh clams, snails, prawns
Beche-de-Mer, octopus, squid.

Cages of ducks and pigeons
live dogs, civitcats, and
snakes of a dozen kinds.
Like a specialized zoo.

Containers or aquariums and bags with fish
I had never seen outside of a textbook.

In windows hang smoked ducks and
pieces of fresh and smoked meat,
congee and medicinal soups.

Food is cheap but not living space

*****

Victoria Peak

We found the Victoria Peak tram station
on Garden Road.
The three-hour coolie-operated sedan chairs
were replaced in 1888
with a tram that took 8 minutes
to Peak Tower with its
 souvenir shops,
 restaurant,
 post office and
 viewing deck.

The ride was from a James Bond movie
past prestigious homes and tropical vegetation.
From the top we could see
 islands of the South China Sea,
 and the New Territories.

Time rules and we took the tram back down.
If time could be slowed there was:
 the walk up Mount Austin Road;
 Victoria Peak Gardens;
 Pok Fu Lam Country Park.

So much to see and so few lifetimes.

*****

Long March Tea House

This was years back
when the Kuo Ming Tang
chased Mao on his Long March

Early morning in a small village in Schezuan
several KMT soldiers
came into a mountain tea house
on a cold, cold morning.

They warily eyed the other customers
in the small dark building in the mountains
and drank from house supplied cups.
Some other customers had their own cups
and looked like woodcutters and farmers.

They spoke different dialects in their groups.
finishing tea and hands warm they all
bowed to each other and exited the tea house
each group in a different direction.
Each group quickly disappeared into the woods.

An hour later the shooting began again.

*****

Taiwan
or is it
Formosa

By
Carl Lahser

Dedication

Yeh Chi Fu, an old friend from Taiwan (Formosa?), insisted that he was from the independent island of Formosa. He remembered the Americans bombing his village during WWII when the island was occupied by the Japanese. He spoke Japanese well as well as the Cantonese dialect of Chinese and some Haka. He and his friends in the Formosan Student Association had no use for Chang Kai-shek.

Taiwan or is it Formosa
July 1981

While stationed on Guam we decided to visit Taiwan. We had access to space available military transportation and found a flight headed for Japan. We drove to Andersen AFB and left the car with a friend in family housing who took us to base operation. A C-130 cargo plane took us to Tokyo where we could see Mt Fuji in the distance. A couple hours later we got a hop to NS Kadena on Okinawa on the south end of Japan.

The "we" included my wife, Carol, our eleven year old son, Charles, and myself. I was a civilian environmental engineer working for the Navy Public Works Center on Guam.

We were lucky enough to get transit quarters for the night and a reservation on the ferry to Keelung, Taiwan, the next evening. Since we had military ID cards we went off base for some tourist shopping - China Pete and a couple others.

We had supper at a local Japanese restaurant before heading back to the base. I had sushi served on the scrupulously clean counter top. Charles and Carol shared a steak and bowls of rice. I noticed several vending machines that sold hot tea and coffee and noodle soup or cold sodas and even wine and hot saki,

Polution

Next afternoon we took a taxi to the port of Naha to board the ferry. It was an overnight trip. We had an outside cabin with a little veranda. The trip was one of those "magic" nights with a near full moon shining over the South China Sea. Supper and breakfast were purchased in the ship's cafeteria. Our son was not impressed. He was bored with watching the sea and reading stories and annoyed that some of the Chinese wanted to pat a little blond-headed boy on the head for good luck.

Late in the afternoon about three hours from Keelung trash and oil slicks began to appear. This flotsam got thicker as we approached land.

We docked about sundown, went through customs and caught a cab to the Imperial Hotel about 15 miles towards Taipei.

I had heard that the Imperial Hotel, No. 600 Lin Shen North Road, Taipei City, was an old hotel. It was built in the 1960s by Madame Chang as a 5-star hotel. Our room had teak floors and furniture with a breeze through the curtained windows.

It was dark by the time we checked in. After checking out the room we headed for one of the hotel restaurants. We ordered dinner. It was slow in coming and Charles was asleep with his head on the table

Imperial Hotel

before we were served.

Next morning we took a taxi to the airport to catch a mid morning plane for a 25 minute flight to Hualein on the east coast about half way down the island. We had booked a two day tour of Taroko Gorge, Taichung, Sun Moon Lake, and a bus back to Taipei.

After a 25 km ride to the bus station we boarded the bus with several Chinese and Japanese tourists. The road followed the Liwu River and along the edge of Toroko (marble) Gorge. There had been efforts made to mine the marble or dam the gorge for power generation but the government had made it into a national park.

This road was two lanes wide in places and much less in most. We passed truck traffic with part of our tires over thin air a couple hundred feet above the river. The passengers were encouraged to sing so we got a variety of Chinese and Japanese. Even Charles sang one for the crowd.

Taroko Gorge

Taroko Gate

Liwu River

Orchards

The trip began at the Taroko Gate and passed Park Police Hostel and several small tunnels.After about an hour we left the gorge behind. We

Budha at PaoChuehTemple

passed through several tunnels on the way to the top of the mountain range. There was a hour stop for lunch near Lishan.

We began cruising down the switchbacks with narrow terraced orchards of apple and pear trees espaliered against the against the mountain side.

There was a stop at the PaoCueh Temple near Taichung where we took a break and toured the facility. I bought several water color pictures done by the monks. There was a fruit stand where I bought a kilo of leeches'. I ate leeches' for a couple days and there were still fruit left.

We arrived at Sun Moon Lake and checked in at a

hotel for the night. Sun Moon Lake is the largest natural lake (7.7 sq Km) in Taiwan. It is a figure eight with Guanghua Island between the north and south portions. The lake with a average depth of 40 meters is nestled between Mt. Shuiset and Mt. Dajiae. It is famous as a honeymoon destination.

The Road to Sun Moon Lake passed the Wen Wu Taoist Temple near Puli with a collection of life-sized statues of the Immortals and the Monkey King. We stopped to see the temple and get a first good look at the lake.

Next stop was the Sun Moon Hotel. We checked in and walked along the beach to a Formosan Ami village where the Taroko First Nation aboriginals put on demonstrations of song and dance and sold crafts much like some of the US and Canadian First Nation Indian tribes. They came to Formosa about 8000 years ago and first encountered outsiders when the Han dynasty Chinese began to settle the island in the 17th century. The total population of these Austronesian natives is about a half a million. These aborigines are subject to social and economic discrimination.

Immortals at Wen Wu Temple

Charles and the Monkey King

At supper Charles did not like anything on the menu except rice and upset the waiter when he put soy sauce on his rice. That was not the way Taiwanese ate their rice!

Next morning we continued down innumerable switchbacks through forests of camphor and pine trees to Shuli and Changhua. An outstanding feature was the bicycles outnumbered all other types of transportation with motorcycles and scooters coming in second. Another surprise was the use of every square inch of land for agriculture. There were gardens between buildings and in vacant lots and in pots in the windows.

Wen Wu Temple   Charles and the Ami

We left the Sun Moon Lake area on a relatively modern road heading back to Taipei a little after lunch and arrived in mid afternoon.

We found a newer and less expensive hotel in downtown Taipei. We took a tour of the city and spent a afternoon at Elephant Mountain Park.

When we returned to the room we found that Carol's jade ring had been stolen. The local cops said it would probably not be recovered. Next morning the person who had cleaned our room did not show up for work. .

Our last day was spent visiting a couple museums showing Chinese art and antiques that Chiang Kai-Shek had liberated from mainland China.

We were out to the airport at sunup for a flight back to Okinawa. It seemed strange to ride through the blacked out city and airport. The government was paranoid about being attacked and used the black out to get the population involved. We sat in the empty terminal as the sun came up and other passengers began to arrive. The flight left about 0900.

Back at Kadena we checked with flight operations for a flight back to Guam. They said there was one scheduled the next day and that we would have to get a Philippine visa in case we would have to stop in the Philippines on the way home. This would entail a taxi ride into Naha the next day to see the honorary Philippine consulate, a local businessman.

We checked in at the transient quarters and went to the beach for the afternoon Next morning we found the consulate. He took the information for the visas, charged us $30 each, and told us to be back after lunch.

We shopped in downtown and had lunch. About 1400 we went back to the consulate to pick up our visas and took a taxi back to the main gate area where we did some more shopping.

I left Carol and Charles at the room and went to see operations about a hop. A C-130 was leaving early next morning. We left at 0700 next morning and after a 6 hour flight were back on Guam.

Home from traveling its time to write up my notes before I forget.
Was it Taiwan or Formosa?

China Visit

April 2006
Carl and Carol Lahser

On 19 April 2006, we returned from our trip to China. The experience was worth the time and expense. Although China was not the China of Terry and the Pirates it was not the Red Guard China either. The China we saw was a dynamic and evolving society, no longer a third world country. My trip report follows.

The Dream.

In June 2003, we discussed a trip to China listed in the Viking Tours brochure. We signed up in December 2004 for a trip in mid-April to avoid cold weather. The trip would extend from Beijing, through several cities and down the Yangtze ending in Hong Kong. Estimated cost $9,000.

Several months later, I found the trip had been turned around and scheduled to obtain another day in Hong Kong. Trip would be 4 – 20 April 2006. This was actually better since it allowed two more weeks for Beijing to warm up. The new schedule would begin in Hong Kong, a flight to Guilin in Guangxi province with a trip on the Li River through zen mountains, a flight to Shanghai, another flight to Yi Chang for a three day trip up the Yangtze River, including the Three Gorges Dam, Xiling Gorge, the Wu and Qutang Gorges, a stop at Fengdu, then a short sail to Chongqing (formerly Chungking) in Sichuan province, a flight to Xian in Shaanxi province (former capitol of the Qin dynasty), and a flight to Beijing (Old Peking). Somewhere a decision had been made to fly DFW/Hong Kong and Beijing/DFW with no connection between San Antonio and DFW. This was supposed to save a few bucks but required a flight to and from DFW but added two night's hotel in Dallas.

Itemized cost is:

American Airlines San Antonio to DFW and return	$ 200
Holiday Inn DFW two nights	$ 156
United Airlines DFW/Hong Kong – Beijing/DFW	$ 2,120
Hong Kong/Guilin extension	$ 2,596
Land tour	$ 3,360
Inter-Asia Air Taxes	$ 38
Yangtze cruise	$ 1,398
Total	$ 9,842

Then there will be tips and purchases

Background.

Back in ancient times (1940's) I learned of China from reading Terry and the Pirates in the Sunday comics. Somewhere in the back of my mind was a desire to see Hong Kong, Rangoon, and Shanghai.

We lived on Guam from 1978-82. In 1979, my mother-in-law decided to drop by from Texas and offered to split the cost for a trip to Hong Kong and Macao. We spent ten days and had a wonderful time. During our almost four years on Guam, we also visited Taiwan, Okinawa, and Korea. It will be interesting to see how Hong Kong has changed.

Getting Ready.

We began preparations. For me the planning and preparation for a trip like this is fun and a learning experience in itself. It is an important part of any trip. Of course, like an old English traveler said, if you do your research well there is really no reason to visit exotic places. Possible but I will still go if I get the opportunity.

I would make a chronological picture picture record and chronological tape recordings to create a trip report. I would add lists of birds I saw and plants I identified. Most would be identified on site while others woul be identified from pictures. Many of the plants would be ornamentals. Birds would be recorded where seen. Hopefully there will be some trips out of towns.

To check out the current political situation in China I called the Air Force Office of Special Investigations (AFOSI) and got their anti-terrorism brief. I next checked medical area intelligence reports. These reports consisted of the Disease Vector Ecology Profile (DVEP) prepared by the Defense Pest Management Information Center and the Monthly Disease Occurrence (Worldwide) from the Armed Forces Medical Information Center. I also called the Communicable Disease Center (CDC) Malaria Hotline [(404) 639-1610]. The malaria people said malaria should not be a problem, but there were reported cases of dengue fever. The CDC said there were no appreciable disease problems and recommended only normal shots.

Out came my old Mandarin course texts and tapes for review. I bought a portable language translator, a Lingo ten language that included Chinese and extra batteries. Practice with the translator showed it was difficult to use, had a limited vocabulary of words and phrases and was, in general, not particularly useful. It was left behind.

I got more memory chips for my digital cameras. I also bought rechargeable batteries and a new fast charger. This would give me capacity for about 2500 pictures. I also picked up new tapes for my old analog tape recorder.

When I had donated a collection of over a hundred volumes on Chinese culture and history to the Witte Museum to support a new oriental history wing I had kept a couple guides to China as general reference. I picked up several more current visitor guides and some new reference books on birds and plants of Asia. These included:

Lonely Planet guides to *China, Beijing, Hong Kong* and *Taiwan;*
China Guidebook by Kaplan and de Keijzer;
Hong Kong at Cost by Wilson,
An Eye on Hong Kong by Keith Macgregor,
a picture book of Hong Kong, Kowloon and Macao,
China Diary by Spender and Hockney;
Beautiful Kweilin.

I also rounded up several natural resources books:

Hong Kong Birds by Viney and Phillipps;
Birds of Southeast Asia by Strange;
A Birders checklist of the Birds of Hong Kong by Sargeant;
Tropical Plants of Southeast Asia by an unlisted author;
Handy Pocket Guide to Tropical Plants by E. Chan;
A Field Guide to Tropical Plants of Asia by David Engel;
Plant Life of the Pacific World by Elmer Merrill;
Alpine Plants of China by Zhang.

There were also a number of Internet sites on plants, seashells, and butterflies of China, Manchuria, Korea and Vietnam, Singapore, Malaysia, and the Philippines.

I found slides from the previous trip to Hong Kong and Macao and scanned them into the computer. There were almost 400 pictures that I had shot or bought or otherwise obtained. What else should a retiree do?

Applications for China visas cost $98 each by courier.

In mid March we got the trip papers including tickets and itinerary. I got my window seat and Carol got her aisle for the 12-hour flight over the pole. We were scheduled to go to Hong Kong first. This would allow another week for Beijing to warm up. Hong Kong would be in the 70's and Beijing still in the 50's with blowing yellow sand.

Weight limitations were a pain. United Airlines allowed two 50-pound suit cases each plus a carryon but the inter-China flights were limited to 44 pounds for one suitcase and an 11-pound carryon. My take-along references were limited to the *Lonely Planet China Survival* Kit and *Birds of Southeast Asia*. This also eliminated some clothes we would probably not wear anyway.

By departure time I had absorbed all the Mandarin I could stand and felt that I might be able to understand some and maybe speak a little.

By noon on 3 April we were ready?

To Hong Kong

Monday, 3 Apr 2006. We left home about 1300 for the airport. We checked in at the American desk and flew to DFW. After a night at the la Quinta Baymont motel near the airport at Bedford, we took the 0500 Shuttle to the airport. La Quinta had sold the Baymont chain. It was an old run down facility that was not ADA compliant and probably would not meet current building codes. The room telephone was inoperative along with other deficiencies.

Tuesday, 4 Apr 2006. We checked in with United Airline for a flight to Chicago O'Hare and on to Hong Kong. We left warm DFW about 0800 and arrived at a chilly O'Hare about 1000 after a smooth flight. Our connecting flight was at 1130 with immigration and customs to keep us occupied.

I was in seat 57A on a 747-400. The flight was 7782 miles in about 14 hours flying time. Route was over Rockford, IL, across Wisconsin to Cheguamegon Bay and across Lake Superior, over the eastern tip of Minnesota and across snowy Ontario where the rivers ran north to near Ft. Severn on Hudson's Bay. We crossed several lakes where ice logging roads crossed the lake.

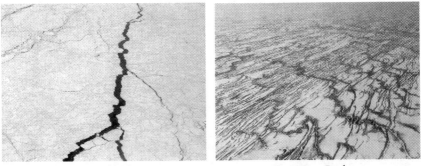

Open leads   Pressure Ridges

We crossed a frozen Hudson's Bay to about Southampton Island, over the Booth Peninsula and the Gulf of Boothia, the M'Clure Strait, the Queen Elizabeth Islands to about 77° North or about 400 miles from the North Pole, then out over the Beaufort Sea and Arctic Ocean. Pressure ridges open leads and a few ice islands were below. We passed over the

East Siberian Sea south of Ostrov Novaya Sabir and dirty brown sea ice. Landfall was between the Indigirka and Yana Rivers flying west along the coast to the Lena R. delta. It surprised me to see so much humanity this far north. Long straight roads, strip mines, clear-cut timber stands, and tree farms. I was told that the roads were the old Soviet military security system. Some of the rivers had loading areas, and one had a tug and barges breaking the ice. The taiga forest was the remains of the largest continuous forest in the world. It was larger than the state of Alaska. The record low temperature was -94°F with -50°F a common winter temperature. This is the home of a primitive wild horse and the endangered musk deer and a group of natives who herd reindeer.

A thousand miles south began the Siberian steppes, the home of the Goiter Gazelle and wild camels. There were small isolated lakes like prairie potholes called huttogs. We flew up the Lena valley to about Zhigansk in the Russian State of Sakha and saw the Trans Siberian RR tracks then flew over some really rough mountains sprouting to over 15,000 feet passing just east of Lake Baykal.

Near Ulan Ude we turned south over the Hentuyn Nuruu Mountains in clouds near Ulaanbaatar in Mongolia then crossed the flat Gobi Desert. There were with a few potholes and a railroad running southeastwards towards Beijing. Air temperature was –58° F. Sand changed from light tan to a darker brown.

Entering Inner Mongolia near Baoton we crossed the Great Wall of China not visible from the air. Further south, we passed east of Xi'an and crossed the Yangtze near Yi Chang. Just west of Guangzhou (formerly Canton) we turned east to Hong Kong (officially Xiangtan) and landed near sunset. We had been in daylight for the entire flight otherwise. They had fed us two big meals plus snacks and Chinese noodles and about every hour they passed by with water or juice.

We landed at the new airport on Lantau Island (Tai Yue Shan) about 25 miles west of downtown. The airport is built on fill so they have strict weight limits. There were seven million people in HK now and lots of landfill material.

Our guide pointed out significant landmarks and briefed us on our stay in the Kowloon/Hong Kong/Lantau area. We passed a big container port and flew along the North Lantau Expressway towards

New Airport   Hurricane Harbor Hong Kong

Downtown crossing the Kap Shui Mun Bridge and Ma Wan Island. The trip continued across the Tsing Ma Bridge and Tsing Yi Island and along freeways to the Hung Hom district of Kowloon to the five-star Shangri-La Hotel. Everyone wants to live in downtown. All 7.5 million. Good thing that only about 5% have private cars.

We checked in and the room steward delivered our luggage and a pot of tea. He also delivered a couple apples with a knife since most Orientals cut apples instead of taking a bite out of them. The room on the eleventh floor was large (25X56 ft) with nice bath, refrigerator, a safe, terry cloth robes and slippers, all kinds of goodies. It had a TV with all Chinese stations. There were two double beds with duvets that were either hot or cold depending on where the thermostat was set. The hotel usually ran about $350 a night.

Supper was in the hotel's Shang restaurant. It was European style ala Carte where even the rice ($6) was ordered separately.

After supper (dinner at those prices), we went for a walk around the immediate area. It was overcast, and 6°C (upper 40's). I was surprised me with the number of safety posters in Chinese and English at a construction site next door including a Dengue Fever warning sign. The subways were new and there was a subway entrance near the hotel. I shot several pictures and returned to the room.

I asked about the availability of the old Chinese breakfast. I was told that this was modern China and a first class hotel so I was surprised by the availability of congee, thousand year eggs, and other ingredients for the old style breakfast in any hotel.

Wednesday, 5 April 2006. About 0630, I went down to the hotel's Café Cool by myself. This facility stretched along the side of the hotel overlooking the harbor. It could seat about 150 and served from eight island stations like pastry, cold like sushi, hot like eggs and pancakes, Japanese dishes, fruit and cereal.

I asked if breakfast was ready and was told it opened at 0600 but was not ready yet but have a table. They brought me a cup of tea, which was really dark and strong. I had hoped I would get good tea in China so I commented on this. The waitress explained they had one pot and that many people like strong tea. However, I could order a pot of special tea so I did. It was a pot of water with the tea bag in it and another pot of water I could dilute it if the tea was too strong. I had a choice of Jasmine or green tea.

Breakfast was outstanding: Lots of fruit – lichees, jackfruit, oranges, pineapple, papaya, mango, and strawberries; Japanese – miso, sashimi, sushi, pickled vegetables, grilled tomatoes, grilled fish; Chinese – various but included congee and trimmings; American - waffles, rolls, scrambled eggs, omelets, cereal. I was tempted to try it all. Congee, shrimp rolls, custard buns, fresh salmon sashimi, and fried pomfrit were enough to start with.

About 0700, I took a chilly walk down Mody Road to Nathan Road then down to the clock tower at the Star Ferry terminal and back – about 2 KM or 1.5 miles. There had been a lot of changes. The open market on Mody Road was gone replaced by a zillion small shops. Nathan Road was a four-lane divided street instead of a simple two lanes. Kowloon City Park was now covered with a mall and a new mosque instead of trees. No more big jewelry stores with gold statues and armed guards on the door. These had been replaced by numerous small shops. The Star Ferry terminal has expanded to include a bus terminal. The clock tower has been cleaned up and made into a park. Kai Tak airport had disappeared into the harbor. The whole waterfront, now called the Promenade, had been modified by urban renewal with several museums and a theatre, a conference center and hotel and a Walk of Movie Stars along the water. Buildings like the YMCA, Peninsula Hotel, and Seamen's Club were still there but no longer across the street from the Kai Tak terminal.

Many of the street crossings had audio signals plus countdown for the crossing. Pedestrian crossings under the main streets were called subways.

Construction sites had changed. They still used bamboo up to about 60 floors. Now the bamboo was draped with plastic sheeting and there was a safety net about every five floors and elevators instead of stairs. Rooftop cranes were all over town.

I walked through the park in front of the art museum on the Promenade. Only one old man was doing Ti Chi when there had been hundreds of senior citizens in the city park in 1979.

Construction Site   Warning Poster

Tropical vegetation included trees like the Lettuce Tree (Pisonia alba), Flamboyant or Royal Poinciana (Delonix regia), Bottlebrush (Callistemon lanceolatus), Australian Pine (Auracaria heterophylla), Geiger Tree (Cordia sebestena), African Tulip Tree (Spatheodea campanulata), Hong Kong Orchid Tree (Bauhinia purpurea), Fiddlewood (Citharexylum spinosum), and shrubs like Ixoria (Ixoria spp.), Lantana (Lantana sp.), Plumbago (Plumbago sp.), Banana (Musa spp.), and Oleander (Nerium spp.). There were also palms – Manila palms, Fish tail Palms (Caryota mitis), Madagascar Palm (Chrysalidocarpus lutescens), Hurricane Palm (Ptychosperma macarthurii), Chinese Fan Palm (Livistona chinensis).

Few birds were seen and only in the parks. Birds included a pair of Spotted Doves (Streptopelia chinensis), a Brown Shrike (Lanius cristatus), several Red-Whiskered Bulbuls (Pycnonotus jocosus), and a single Eurasian Tree Sparrow (Passer montanus). I neither saw nor heard a gull of any kind. I returned to the Shangri-La Hotel in time for a tour of Hong Kong.

Victoria Peak. About 0900, we loaded up the bus for the tour of HK, flew up Mody Road and dove into the new Cross Harbor Tunnel surfacing near the Royal HK Yacht Club on HK Island. We drove along the Henessy Road freeway bypassing Wanchai and Central Districts and up serpentine Findley Road to Victoria Station. The tram to the top of the hill was closed for some reason. When we were here in 1979, we rode the tram the 1200m to the Peak Tower. It was an interesting ride up a steep slope on a cog rail tram. The tram ride was about 15 minutes. Prior to 1888 the ride to the top for a proper Englishman in a sedan chair with four coolies took about three hours.

I asked about some of the hutongs like Cat Street (where an old woman had refused to sell my son a red jacket in 1979 because red was a girl's color) and about the Street of the Thousand Year Egg (where fertile duck eggs baked in vats of hot ashes). These were in Wangchai and, although the street names still existed, the hutongs (old apartment complexes) had been eliminated and replaced by new condos. I also asked about the Tiger Balm Garden (officially known as the Aw Boon Haw Gardens) where my son had intentionally gotten lost so he could spend more time exploring the wonders. I was told they had gone bankrupt and been sold to Mr. Lee, a local billionaire.

High priced homes and cars cover the hill. Thick vegetation with bamboo and broadleaf trees lined the road and screened the homes. We passed the old tram keeper's home and walked around to the backside of the hill that overlooked the harbor.

Tram keeper's home   Hurricane Anchorage from Peak

Several Red-Whiskered Bulbuls (<u>Pycnonotus</u> <u>jocosus</u>) were playing in the brush. A couple Eastern Marsh-Harriers (<u>Circus</u> <u>spilonotus</u>) were riding the thermals. Wild cane and yellow lantana were the primary cover. Indian Laurel (Calophyllum inophyllum) clumps were present. Common weeds included a Purple Oxallis, a Yellow Oxallis, white lantana, and several small composites. A green dragon fly and several butterflies that looked like cabbage butterflies flitted about. The guides told of the various buildings that followed feng schui (or not) and the luck of the building owners.

On the way down, we passed a vendor who was selling digital pictures. He had a battery and inverter hooked to a camera, a laptop and a digital printer.

We stopped at the landing where the Victoria Peak Station (now, Peak Galleria) was undergoing renovation. Another shopping center with a Thai restaurant and an ice cream shop were thriving. Fifty-eight $HK for ice cream?! That was almost $8 US. And I thought Ben and Jerry's prices were high.

Repulse Bay is on the south side of HK Island and named for a British man-of-war. It was clean and deserted on this Wednesday. We only saw the bay and the Tin Hau temple built by the Life Saver's Club. There were two large statues - Tin Hau and Kwun Yum - all decorated in Mandarin style. The beach is also called "Be No" Beach for its list of restrictions.

There were Red-Whiskered Bulbuls and several Crested Mynas (Acridotheres cristatellus) in the beach landscaping.

Repulse Beach   Be-No sign

The next stop was Aberdeen at the landing for the floating restaurants. The floating restaurants, Jumbo and Tai Pak, no longer took walk-ins. Any harbor was full of yachts. And we did not see the boat people.

Ap Lei Chau (Duck's Tongue) or Aberdeen Island was covered with high rise condos and public housing renting for about $100/mo for an apartment less than 100 square feet.

I saw a pair of Black Kites (<u>Milvus</u> <u>migrans</u>) cruising the harbor.

Aberdeen Harbor   Floating Restaurant Landing

The Golden Bauhinia Plaza was the last stop on HK Island. It was a gift from the Chinese government built on the island waterfront as a memorial to HK rejoining China. There is a giant golden Bauhinia or HK orchid in the center. The orchid was clearly visible across the harbor from out hotel.

The group returned to the hotel after lunch. Carol and I went out to a recommended Dim Sum restaurant. Not the variety I expected and, at $5 an item, way too expensive.

We walked down to Nathan Road dodging businessmen wanting to sell us custom made clothing, $29 Rolex watches, and all kinds of jewelry. We found a shop and bought a nice digital camera. We also found a shop specializing in pearls and bought a nice necklace and earrings. Many of the sales people spoke very good English but then most of these kids had been raised under British rule.

We went down to the Promenade about 8PM to watch the laser show. Several large buildings on HK Island had lasers on top and music was coordinated along the Promenade. The evening was overcast with low clouds and the show was probably as good as could be.

After the laser show, we found a McDonald's for supper. I tried a Korean flatbread sandwich and Carol had a cheeseburger with fries. Interesting. There were about 300 McDonald franchises and about the same number of Kentucky Fried Chicken franchises in China. Lots of Starbucks too.

Promenade

Promenade Movie Star Statues

7-11 Store

Starbucks

Thursday, 6 April 2006. Breakfast for me was fried salmon, taro buns, sushi, sashimi, plain congee with a thousand-year egg and my special tea. Then I over indulged with a Yankee-style jelly doughnut and fresh fruit. I try a little bit of a lot of things, but I gotta watch it.

We had a free day to shop and look around. We began about 0900 walking down the Promenade looking at the walk of stars. We went to the art museum. There was a modern art exhibit, a contemporary Chinese exhibit and an exhibit of new Chinese artists.

Carol wanted to head back for the hotel so we stopped at McDonald's again and at a supermarket to pick up some diet Cokes. Market space was contracted by several vendors instead of being owned by one big company.

Carol crashed and I took off again looking for our hotel from the previous trip and the Yue Hwa store. I walked down to Nathan Road and turned west (inland) and found the Miramar Hotel where we had stayed for ten days in 1979. It was being renovated into condos.

I followed the map to the Yue Hwa store. In 1979, it was a first class PRC (mainland China) outlet and department store. Today, it was old and tired. The goods were nothing special. Most of the clothing was out of date. I was disappointed since this was once the official Chinese government outlet.

The new Harbor City Mall was about a block away. Three stories high, four blocks long, and two blocks wide and filled with modern boutiques and specialty shops. Carol had asked about a bookstore and I found one. I looked around at electronic equipment. I finally found a shop with a digital micro recorder that I bought. Its price started out at $95 and I bought it for $70.

On returning to the hotel I told Carol about Harbor City and she was quickly ready to go shop. She wanted to take a cab the five blocks I guess to so she could save up for the 2-3 miles walking in the Mall. We looked at books and shoes and clothes and Chinese home appliances and electronics. Interesting items included electric tea kettles, cubic foot refrigerators, and portable air conditioners. We finally walked back to the hotel to crash.

Friday, 7 April 2006. My breakfast was congee and miso with fresh fruit and tea. See? I already cut back.

We had until 1230 to shop before going to the airport for the flight to Guilin. We had our bags out in the hall ready for an 1130 pickup and went last minute shopping about 0930 when things were just opening. All the portable displays were being moved out onto already crowded sidewalks. If you looked at anything they expect a sale since the first customer must buy something or its bad luck for the day. We got an opening deal on some freshwater pearls. Almost like the Korean War saying, "One time good deal, G.I." We looked at jade and went through The Opal Mine and the changes to Nathan Road and headed back to the hotel. I stopped to look at a fruit shop that had grapes, anona, pomellos, papaya, oranges, and apples.

I was amazed at the number of people out along the street. When I was out about 0800 in 1979 it was just me, the binjo man, and maybe a couple others. Now a big percentage of the people had MP-3 players or cell phones plugged into their ears.

There were a bunch of young US sailors from the US aircraft carrier CVAN Abraham Lincoln. They looked just like young sailors on liberty used to look. Some things don't change much.

We passed an art gallery I had passed several times. Father and son artists had a couple hundred oil paintings on display mostly done quickly with palette knife. We chose a HK street scene and a modern painting. These were 20X24 inches and costing about $80 US or about $0.16/sq. in. US sale prices begin about $3/sq. in. to break even and make minimum wage. They rolled and wrapped the canvases nicely and we went back to the hotel to repack.

I was surprised at the cleanliness of the streets. There seemed to be a street sweeper in sight somewhere every time I went out.

We went to the hotel's Café Cool and had burgers and cokes for $50. Good food but higher prices than at the airport.

About 300 cars per day were being added to HK's existing million autos. Obtaining a HK driver's license required several tests over several years plus about $2000 US. The automobile injury death rate had increased by 300% in the past ten years.

A dog license costs about $800 plus $200 a year. We saw a few dogs on leashes.

I discussed energy efficiency with our guide. Water costs about $4/ cu.meter. They also circulate grey water for toilet flushing and you can be fined for using drinking water to flush. Shops with air conditioning use sliding doors or revolving doors but most still use regular swinging doors that lose a lot of cold air. Appliances are small and energy efficient. Our guide said he did not need a remote for the TV; his apartment was so small he could change channels with his toes from bed.

Warning Sign   Street Crossing

The hotel elevator required the room key to take us to our floor. Even the elevators think they are smarter than I. Some hotels required the key card be inserted in a slot by the door to turn the lights on.

Some of the translations of Chinese street signs were a little strange. One instructed you not to annoy the birds. Another sign said to stay in the cross walks or you would be persecuted immediately. Then there were the diverted pedestrians.

When we were leaving Carol changed some traveler's checks for Chinese Yuan but had to change US dollars to HK dollars first. The HK dollar was $0.02 difference from the Yuan. They are looking for parity in a couple years.

We discussed real estate. The West has taught China about different ways to buy a house and different kinds of loans like fixed rate and balloon payments. Aren't they lucky? Apartments were sold by the square meter (about 10 sq ft). Prices run from $400 – $1,000 per square meter with rooms as small as 10 sq meters (110 sq ft).

Guilin. We went out to the airport about 1600 and flew to the autonomous region of Guilin. Our 1800 one-hour flight got off at 1900. It was raining so I put the camera up and slept.

It was a smooth ride with a few bumps on let down. We landed about 2030 in the rain. Next was a 45-minute trip to the Sheraton Guilin hotel on the west bank of the Li River. First thing to see out of the terminal was a large green and pink neon palm tree.

Our guide said Guilin or Kweilin (Forest of Sweet Osmanthus) was a new model town that had been torn down and rebuilt. Several 5-star and other levels of guesthouses were built and Guilin was receiving about five million tourists a year.

Guilin was an autonomous region where the natives pay no taxes and the region rules itself. There were ten tribes or minorities in this region including Mong and Meo. The Chinese population is made up of 56 tribes with the Han being the dominant. These tribes are much like our Native American tribes.

Guilin was founded in the Qin dynasty (221-206 BC) as a focal point to control the Ling Canal that had been constructed in 214 BC. The 25-mile canal connected the Likiang tributary of the Pearl River and the Hsiangliang tributary of the Yangtze Rivers. It became a provincial capitol under the Ming dynasty until the capitol was moved to Nanking in 1914. It was a Communist stronghold during the 1930s and WWII when the population peaked at over a million.

Guilin manufactured pharmaceuticals and chemicals and had a bus assembly plant and an engine factory at the local prison. Guilin is only about 200 miles from Vietnam and trades with Vietnam for agriculture.

I went down to the hotel bar about 2300 and tried a local beer called "Ligan". It smelled strange but tasted good. It was served with salted peanuts instead of roasted soy beans.

Guilin was home of Osmanthus and green tea products and a liquor called "Quewhan". Osmanthus (Osmanthus aurantiacus or O. fragrans) is in the Oleaceae family with opposite, spiny, entire leaves and clusters of yellow, white or orange flowers. Petals are harvested and used to make the tea and liquor. Other local fermented products include a three-flower wine, a grape wine, and a whiskey.

There was a live piano player spotlighted in red. Strings of yellow lights lined the handrails and steps up to the dining room on the mezzanine overlooking the lobby. Maybe they like garish colors locally or they may think tourist like them.

I paid my bill and stopped at the hotel gift shop. They had the Osmanthus products and I bought a package of Osmanthus tea, which I am drinking as I write. The gift shop had a good selection of Chinese products like cloisonné, cinnabar, wood and stone carvings, jade and other stone jewelry, and guide books. I asked about antiques and was told they could not export antiques over 200 years old but they had a good selection of middle and late Ch'ing artifacts. They opened at 0700 so Carol could look before we left for the river trip.

Schedule was 0700 for breakfast. We were to checkout about 0800 and load up on the bus for a half hour ride to the embarkation point for the Li River trip through karst mountains that look like Zen paintings. We would take a three-hour's ride downstream including lunch and be at Yangshou by mid afternoon. It would be a two-hour trip back to Guilin, dinner, and a plane to Shanghi.

Time to crash.

Saturday, 8 April 2006. We were down for breakfast about 0700. Everything from the previous breakfasts was available plus a local specialty, fermented bean curd. The guide called it Chinese Limburger. I thought it was really pretty good. There was also small deep fried fish that I liked.

I walked across the street to the Li or Likiang River, a tributary of the Pearl River. The streets, walks and medians were well maintained. A man with an orange jacket and a wide pointed farmers straw hat was sweeping the sidewalk with a brush broom. A fisherman floated past on a bamboo raft. There was a swimmer headed across the river and a man rowing a racing shell. A man with a black coolie hat carried covered baskets hung from a pole across one shoulder.

Shopping Cart   Fisherman Heading Home

A street sign advertised a fishing show. Two and three-wheeled bikes competed for the street with cycles, three-wheeled trucks, cars, and busses. Some medium-sized birds were high in the trees sounding much like Robins. I saw a Eurasian Tree Finch (<u>Passer</u> <u>montanus</u>). Bark of the trees supported mosses and ferns in the humid air and 72 inches of rain.

We began our bus ride by passing over the river and through the newer part of town. We passed Seven Star Park with its zoo. The seven rounded wooded hills seen from above or on a map were arranged like the big dipper.

The 300-million year old karst hills were scattered throughout town and along the road past the prison and engine factory and golf course to Tujang.

Zen Mountains   Tour Boat

We boarded our boat and found a table on the top deck. There were several other tour boats loading up. Along the shore were bamboo rafts and people collecting water or washing clothes in the river at the landings. Flocks of tame ducks and herds of caribou were frequent sights. The hills were fantastic with rain, sun, fog, and clouds highlighting them. Groins were built in the river to help maintain the channel. Large clumps of tall bamboo (Bambusa vulgaris) were interspersed with terraced farms. Occasional waterfalls cascaded in steps down the hills. Dark karst caves were sites for picnicking and even a couple of boat excursions. Ashoka or Mast Trees (Polyalthia longifolia) grew in solid stands. Blossoms of pink wild plums (Prunus tenella), yellow Osmanthus and white henna (Lawsonia inermis) grew out of the steep jungle walls.

Washing Clothes   Local River Taxis

I saw a Large-billed Crow (Corvus macrorhynchus) and a Black-crowned Night-heron (Nycticorax nycticorax) crossing the river.

Men on bamboo rafts pulled along side to sell produce and trinkets. Water taxis and workboats plied the river. Mong and Meo houses could be seen along the river. At one location, some bamboo rafts had numerous Great Cormorants (Phalacrocorax carbo) used for fishing sunning. They were taken out at night with a collar around their neck to prevent them from swallowing the fish they caught. The birds fished two hours for the fisherman and then were allowed to fish for themselves for an hour.

What appeared to be an Eastern Marsh Harrier (Circus aeruginousus) crossed the river. A White-crowned Forktail (Enicurus leschenaultia) flew to a sand bar at the base of a steep hill.

Lunch was served as we passed Painted Rock. I ordered a plate of fried crab, fish and shrimp in addition to the buffet. Little mud crabs, freshwater Macrobrachium prawns and small unidentifiable fish were all deep fried crisp and good taken with a Tsingtao beer. The buffet was several Chinese dishes like onions and beef, tempura eggplant, and white rice with almond cookies and fruit.

Cormorants   Mud Crabs

A flock of pigeons flew from and circled back to a small village. I saw many pigeons roasted on sticks offered for sale.

We passed several large waterfalls and more caribou and some Mong homes. Terraced farms with grapes, fruit trees, bananas and other crops walked up the hillsides in terraces. Cedars (Toona sinensis) and pines (Pinus Massoniana) grew in patches.

We went ashore at Yang Shou. After a few minutes of bargaining with the "Hello" people we were rescued in golf carts and taken to the bus.

On the way back to Guilin we passed many rice fields with plastic tented rows. There were hot frames of seedling rice. The seedlings would be planted in April and harvested in June. A second crop would be planted in July/August and harvested in October. The second crop was preferred because of the longer growing season. An acre equals six wue and a farmer could handle about 2 wue. Some rice was for food, some for taxes and some for sale.

There were also orchards of oranges and large gourd-shaped pumellos. There were also sugar cane and various berries. Weeds included Brassica, a purple flowered crucifer, and a yellow Oxalis.

Our previous hotel was across the river and difficult to get to with the bus so we stopped at the Ronghu Hotel for a 2-hour break. Many of the group including Carol took advantage of a foot massage while several of us walked around Banyan Lake. The lake was decorated with numerous of Chinese features. There was a number of little cement benches shaped like pigs. One from our group fell down crossing one of the steep arched bridges built for boat traffic.

No handrails. She was luckily not injured.

The landscape plants included Rhododendrons, Cannas, Siberian Irises, Philodendrons, Banyan trees, Oxalis, Weeping Willows, Boxwood, and Creeping Charlie. The whole park was wired with landscape lighting.

We had to go up to street level and cross a major street to get back to the hotel. Lots of bikes, scooters and a few bigger cycles roamed the streets competing with smaller cars and trucks and big busses. One three-wheel bicycle had a refrigerator in the back with a guy holding it on.

Banyan Lake   Guilin Street

Shanghai. We went out for an excellent Chinese supper then were taken to the airport for the plane to Shanghai.

The flight was smooth and wet and the airport was practically down town. We checked in to the Shanghai Hilton right next to the future American Embassy.

Sunday 9 April 2006. The breakfast buffet was very good. One unexpected dish was pork and beans. Chinese? The restaurant was a second-floor-walk-up since the hotel lobby was being renovated and the new American embassy being built next door. It was probably normally a coffee shop and could seat about 100, including two private smoking rooms.

About 0900, we got on the bus for a tour south along Hernan Rd to old Shanghai and the Yuyuan Gardens. The first stop was at the Shanghai Children's Palace. These were schools for exceptional children. The schools were difficult to get in and, even if you were talented, there was a monthly fee. Several students demonstrated their talent on instruments and visual arts. The outside dance recital was moved inside due to rain. We bought several pictures.

The school garden had a beautiful blooming cherry tree, privet hedges, and Ashoka trees.

Shanghai covers about 4,000 sq km while Beijing covers about 7,000. Shanghai's population was about 12 million with the larger Beijing having only 7 million. Wages in Shanghai were higher.

Next stop was the Yuyuan Gardens at the NE end of the old city. We were dropped off in the village square and walked through the drizzle to the garden. This was a 4-acre private garden done in Mandarin style with ponds and bridges, a mountain, temples, etc. This was very intense use of space but still relaxing.

Weeds included Draba, Brassica, and plantains. Ferns and mosses grew on the roof tiles. Cherry trees. Japanese maple. Cedars. Pines. Crepe Myrtle. Wisteria. Weeping Willow.

There was a brief discussion about dragons and Phoenix, male and female. There were water dragons and fire dragons. The males watched after the universe while the females watched the earth. At some point dragons changed and the males became dragons and the females became Phoenix. The number of dragon's toes on the pottery, statues, and clothing indicated the person's rank with the emperor's dragon having five toes on each foot. A mean woman is a dragon woman.

We left the garden and went back to the square with 45 minutes to shop in the Yuyuan bazaar. Looking at several shops I found an art gallery with good original art at ridiculous low prices. Now I have several canvases to stretch and pictures to frame when I get home.

| Shanghai at Night | Silk Rug Weaver |

Lunch was at the New Centaury Hotel. Spicy beef. I tried a Shanghai beer called "Reeb". Good beer. Appears the beer or wine goes with the meal and tea follows it.

After lunch, we stopped at the Bund. This was the Shanghai waterfront and seawall along the Huangpu River. It was flat on top and mostly parks and memorials along street level. The street parallel the Bund was historically Shanghai's Wall Street.

We returned to the hotel to get ready for dinner and a show of folk music and dance. Dinner was at the Motel 168. Large prawns, beef with black pepper, bean curd, BBQ beef, fish with tomato sauce, roasted pork crispy, fried dumplings, sautéed yams and bamboo shoots, seafood soup, fruit, and tea, and Chinese saki.

The entertainment was very professional and enjoyable. I had seen other acrobat groups on Cirq de Soliel, but they were better in real life.

Long day. I had a hard time staying awake.

Monday 10 April 2006. We packed and had the bags out in the hall by 0700. The bus would leave for the airport at 1230.

After breakfast (loquats and thousand year eggs were new additions), we boarded a bus to visit a Shanghai Carpet Factory. Silk begins wrapped around the pupating Silk Moth caterpillar. The pupa is killed in hot water and the silk unwound, spun into thread and yarn, and then dyed. There were murals on the entrance walls depicting the process.

We were shown into the weaving room where weavers were at work. They were busy following patterns. They would put in a knot or two, cut the thread, and begin the next color. Remarkable. A single rug took a few months to a couple years depending in the tightness of the weave, the complexity of the pattern and the size.

In the rug showroom, we saw hundreds of rugs in various patterns and qualities. I had never seen museum quality carpets before - 1600 knots per square inch that looked like paintings. We did not buy anything but others in the party did.

There are street parks and grasslands. Street parks are to use and a lot of people use them for Tai Chi in the morning. Many businesses have their people do Tai Chi, march, or run to show the world they are an aggressive team. The grassland parks are solely for looking at.

An area we did not visit was formerly called New Vienna. This was an enclave of 50,000 European Jews settled in the 1930's. These refugees came to Shanghai because Shanghai did not require any papers. There had been Viennese style homes and nightclubs and German/Austrian music and literature. They had left Austria to avoid going to war and settled in Shanghai just in time for Japanese bombardment.

After lunch, we went to the airport and sat waiting for a China Eastern Airline flight to Yi Chang. China had about 20 airlines flying Boeing 737s or Airbuses. First, the plane was late. Then the flight was cancelled about 1800. We went back to the same hotel for the night.

We had an outstanding Chinese dinner. Chicken special, Cucumber peel, Tiger beer, Beef Special, and fruit for desert. Carol was not impressed and went out for a burger.

I went up to the Sky lounge and shot pictures of the skyline and river. The night sky was clear for a change.

Carol returned to the hotel in a pedicab.

April 2006. We had a free morning and went shopping. The big mall across the street had numerous kiosks and designer outlets. We were picked up at 1100 for the trip to the airport and caught a 1400 plane to Yi Chang.

It was overcast so there was nothing to see enroute. Yi Chang, gateway to the upper Yangtze, was an old walled city first opened to the West in 1877. It was a power generation and water distribution center and they are thinking of piping water to Beijing, a thousand kilometers north. Los Angeles does it. Second biggest industry was tourism.

Yi Chang has a 2400-year history. Located on the border of Sichuan and Hubei provinces it had a population of a million people in town and another 4.5 million in the area. Yi Chang is located at the intersection of the high plateau, the southern plains and the mountains. It was once called Mountain View but was currently called River View. There were 150 tourist agencies in town and a variety of recreational opportunities including white-water rafting, hiking, and other green activities.

We drove out to see the Three Gorges or Ge Zhou Dam in the rain. Below the dam were located a number of cabins and lodges along the river. The river was a blue-green but turned brown in the summer. At the time of our visit the river was about 20m (60 feet) above the historic level.

Three Gorges Lock   Overview of Locks and Dam

After closing the dam and partially filling the lake behind it the downstream sediment load dropped to 20% of preimpoundment levels. This caused a decrease in sediment and nutrient quantities going in to the South China Sea and has cut the diatom population that formed the base of the food chain for one of the largest fisheries in the world. Just imagine what will happen if the Mekong gets its dam. More power, more people, less food.

It was getting on towards evening in the rain. We passed a formation called Chairman Mao Mountain in the Two Step Mountains. It sort of looked like the Chairman lying down.

We passed the first lock traversing the dam. It was a five-step operation up 65m (200 ft) and took 3-8 hours. There were two other locks and a site was prepared to install a ship elevator that would complete the trip in about 2 hours.

They were building 24 generators on site. Each turbine weighs 450 tons. A special bridge had been built to move the generator parts across the dam site for installation. The bridge was rated for 750 tons dead weight and appeared to be working. At this time there were 4500 people working on site. They were housed in an area below the dam - an incentive to do a good job?

We passed the dam as the floodlights were coming on and proceeded by road about 30km up stream in the lower reaches of the Xiling Gorge. At 80km, it was the longest canyon of the Three Gorges.

This was where we boarded our cruise ship. The ship was a year old and after a couple trips through the lock (8-16 hours each) they decided the excitement was just too much and bypassed the dam transit part. (The transit time was about the same as passing through the Panama Canal). Boarding the ship was an adventure of sorts. We boarded a tram for the steep trip dropping 30m from the terminal down to river level. We found our cabin and then went to the dining room for supper and our welcome aboard.

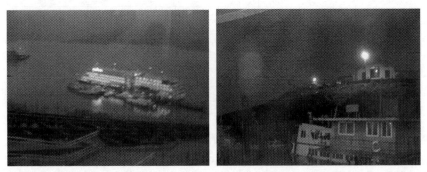

Our Ship on the Yangtze   Loading Terminal

12 April 2006. We stayed in port overnight. About 0530 we cast off and headed up stream. I was up and out about 0700 watching the sunrise, the gorge and other boats on the river. Work boats. Water taxis. Cranes on barges. Container carriers. Tugs with barges of coal. Transporters full of trucks or cars. Barn Swallows (<u>Hirundo</u> <u>rustica</u>) flitted around the ship and across the sundeck. There were large elevator-looking structures of cement plants and large open bunkers where coal was held for loading. Both these facilities had loading chutes or tramways leading from the facility down to the water as much as 100m below. The coal freighters were nasty, dusty black covered with coal dust.

Temperature was about 50°F in mist and an overcast sky. I went in for breakfast, then to the sundeck for Tai Chi.

We sailed the Xiling Gorge with its steep slopes disappearing into the Yangtze that was now about a 100m deep. Numerous caves were still in the hills or had been covered by the river. These were caves where people had hidden from tax collectors and enemies for thousands of years. Some of the caves are covered by as much as 30m of water. Yellow flowered shrubs, Osmanthus (<u>Osmanthus</u> <u>aurantiacus</u>), were conspicuous.

Xiling Gorge   Concrete and Coal Handling

We passed Shenong Stream where numerous coolie "trackers" had once assisted shipping by pulling boats through the rapids.

We stopped over night at Badong in the Wu gorge. There was a good meal and a welcome aboard by the Captain and crew.

We cruised by a city on the south bank. It was the only large city in the gorge and perched high on a hill above the high water line. Old buildings were being dismantled and were strung out downhill into the water. I can't find its name.

13 April 2006. Next morning, we entered the 40km Wu or Wuxia Gorge with lush green misty mountains. All along the river, we had seen houses and villages being disassembled and moved above the high water mark. Several items such as the Kong Ming Tablet at the foot of the Peak of the Immortals were or will be far under water if they cannot be moved. Some of the items have been copied and reinstalled above the high water line or moved to museums.

Vegetation along the river consisted of trees and shrubs including White Spirea (<u>Spirea</u> <u>arborea</u>), and Henna (<u>Lawsonia</u> <u>inermis</u>), Yellow Osmanthus (<u>Osmanthus</u> <u>aurantiacus</u>), and pink wild plum (<u>Prunus</u> <u>tenella</u>). I had no opportunity to see the vegetation closely.

Many of the farms were tilled with the furrows running up and down the hills. Although the government had planted model farms with the rows running along the contours our guide said some farmers did what they wanted in spite of the government examples.

We began passing through the Twelve Peaks. These peaks rose to 900m. The story is that the emperor sent his 12 daughters to defeat a dragon. When they failed they were changed into 12 peaks. One in particular, Goddess Peak, does resemble a female figure.

Hanging Coffin   Goddess Peak

Some of the ridges had fog shrouding the tops. One area had the ridge covered in frost. Waterfalls tumbled out of the fog and mist. Temperature on the river was about 10°C but must have been freezing 300 meters higher.

We stopped at Wushan on the Daning [Da Ning (?)] River to board a smaller cruise ship. This would go up the Daning to the Lesser Three Gorges - up through Dragon Gate Gorge to Misty Gorge into Emerald

Gorge. The Lesser Gorges are a park and the boats and passengers had to purchase tickets. This probably funds the trash boats seen operating on the river picking up floating trash.

Barn Swallows (Hirundo rustica) cruised the river doing circles around the ship. A large long-tailed black bird glided across the river. It fits the description of the Green-Billed Malkoha (Phaenicophaeus tristis). I had heard other birds but could not see them.

Villages Ready to Move   Lunch stop "Hello" people

Near Buddha Mountain in Emerald Gorge, we turned around and stopped at a pavilion for lunch. BBQ chicken, sausage, potato salad that looked more like cottage fries, a brownie and ice tea. We visited the local vendors and I found counterfeit silver dollars amongst other treasures (The woman asked $8 each, then $3, the $1 each and finally three for a dollar). Women lined the stairs selling a variety of foods and goods.

There were Geranium and other common weeds in the rocks along the stairs. Thorny Rubus canes (Rubus palmatus) were growing along the walk.

Down the river I saw a small black bird that fit the description of the Plumbeous Redstart (Rhyacornis fuliginosus). It flew weakly between shrubs at the water's edge at the cliff bottom. Barn Swallows (Hirundo rustica) swept the river for midges. In Dragon Gate Gorge the river color changed from green to brown.

In Dragon Gate Gorge we encountered apes. The local farmers fed the apes to keep the apes out of the fields. We also saw the hanging coffins in caves hundreds of feet above the original river level. Several of these were in the original locations but several had been rescued and placed in museums. Historical hanging foot bridges and plank roads were being flooded and would soon disappear. Square holes for the horizontal supports were cut into the walls. The last foot or so of the handrails were still above water level.

Flooded foot path

Wild Apes

14 Apr 2006. We returned to the ship about 1600. We had a briefing and a guided tour for the last run through the Qutang Gorge. We docked and spent the night tied up.

The exit (or entrance) from the Yangtze valley into the Qutang Gorge was marked by a temple and palace and tower called the White Emperor's City that is not a city and not dedicated to any emperor. The valley widened and numerous coal bunkers and new concrete buildings lined the river.

Mid morning saw us pulling in at Fengdu. We had the option of going to Snow Jade Cave or visiting new Fengdu to see what was left and what would not be inundated. We chose the cave.

A series of switchbacks took us into the hills and out of the Yangtze Valley. Although there were many caves in the area most are small and undeveloped. This one was developed as a tourist destination. There were several Bronzed Drongos (Dicrurus aeneus) claiming stretches of power line along the road.

There was a half-mile incline to the cave entrance and about a mile of developed features in the cave all lit and named. Nice facility.

Something I had never seen before was a two-man palanquin to carry people up or down the sloped walk. They asked $5 each way.

I recognized some of the plants that lined the walk as Ligustrum (Ligustrum sinensis), Mulberry (Morus multicaulis), Philippine Violet Barleria cristata), Grape fern (Botrychium sp), mosses, and liverworts. There were also some large Helix snails.

Two-man Palanquin   Snow Jade Cave

Back on the river, I spotted a gull working along the shallows. Binoculars showed this to be a Common Black-Headed Gull (<u>Larus ridibundus</u>). This was the only gull I saw during the entire trip.

The river valley was widening and there were more farms. Numerous ships hauling coal, machinery, vehicles, and passengers passed heading down stream. There was one location where they were dredging the river and pumping brown spoil into holding ponds on shore. This was the original stream bed and had a decent current up to 12k. For about two hundred years coolie labors, called "trackers", had pulled ships through these rapids and shallows against this current. The water had not backed up this far yet, but there would be a hundred feet of water by 2009.

15 April 2006. Chongqing. We spent the night tied up at Fengdu. The last meal aboard ship was excellent. The Captain and crew were in the receiving line. This was followed by a presentation by local musicians.

Early in the morning, we set out our bags, paid our bill, and left our tips for the crew with the desk. We crossed over a couple intervening barges onto a metal ramp that crossed a mud flat to the stairs leading to the waiting busses.

The local fire department was parked on the gravel at the water's edge washing the trucks and testing the pumps. This was a real Chinese fire drill.

A flock of Barn Swallows (<u>Hirundo</u> <u>rustica</u>) flew around the ship to see us off. A Little Egret (<u>Egretta</u> <u>garzetta</u>) was wading along the in shallow water near some beached barges some distance down stream.

Chongqing Gangway · Real Chinese Fire Drill

Chongqing · "Hello" People Vendors

The "Hello people" were lining the walk and surrounding the busses trying to sell calligraphy sets, folding straw hats, fans and other miscellaneous items. "Hello" appeared to be the only English they knew.

The river had a seawall constructed 85 feet high. I suppose this was their answer to the annual floods and would prevent erosion once the river rises.

Special "Hello people" called stick people wanted to carry our bags on yoke sticks up to the busses for a dollar. They were mostly farmers or descendents of the river trackers. For over a hundred years they had carried produce and other merchandise weighing up to 100 pounds up or down the hundred plus steps of the 85-foot seawall uniting wholesalers and waiting ships. Cranes and conveyors were replacing them on the waterfront but they still roamed the streets. Stick people exist largely because of the numerous steep hills in Chongqing and the low labor rates.

Chongqing dates back to the Ba Kingdom of the Qin Dynasty about 220 BC. It was a trading center located at the juncture of the Jailing River and the Yangtze. It was called Jiangzhou during the Han Dynasty (206 BC to 220 AD) then renamed Yuzhou in the Sui Dynasty ((581-618). Emperor Zhao Dun renamed it Chongqing (double happiness) on the day he became both king and Emperor in 1127. It became a treaty port in 1891. The English name was Chunking.

Stick People   Panda at Zoo

We drove through what the guide called the largest city in the world at 31 million. This must include the surrounding areas or the political district since recent census barely credits Chongqing with 20M.

We arrived at the Chongqing Zoo to see the pandas. I had hoped to see the General Stillwell Flying Tiger museum but was told this was not on the tour partially because the museum, like half of China, was being renovated for the 2008 Olympic visitors. Previous visitors had not been impressed with the museum. The original site was on the flood plain and will be under water.

The entrance to the zoo was through a bamboo forest with three-inch bamboo 30-50 feet tall. We saw three adult Giant Pandas (<u>Ailuropoda melanoleuca</u>) in individual enclosures with plenty of bamboo to eat. They eat the tougher lower parts of the bamboo. A Panda had recently been released into the wild making headlines. There were only a couple hundred in the wild and their reproduction had been very low.

There were also four small red Pandas (<u>Ailuropoda melanoleuca</u>) in an arboreal enclosure since they were tree climbers and eat the tender upper parts of the bamboo plant. A young man with two baskets of bamboo leaves hanging from a pole passed.

Further down the row were large enclosures for tigers. They paced the perimeter probably waiting for a tasty tourist.

A white egret flew over and Red-Whiskered Bulbuls (<u>Pycnonotus jocosus</u>) were tweeting in the trees. Oriental Turtle Doves (<u>Streptopelia orientalis</u>) were perched on branches and feeding along the path. We passed a pond with bamboo trees containing numerous nests and perching Black-crowned Night-herons (<u>Nycticorax nycticorax</u>) and Little Egrets (<u>Egretta garzetta</u>). There was also a pair of tame swans. Beyond the pond were several Common Blackbirds (<u>Turdus merula</u>), Eurasian Tree Sparrows (<u>Passer montanus</u>), and Eye-browed Thrushes (<u>Turdus obscurus</u>). An Azure-winged Magpie (<u>Cyanopica cyanus</u>) was walking along a roof ridge cap. This was the first place in China that I heard many birds calling.

Besides the big bamboos, there were pollarded and espaliered cottonwoods. There were a lot of ornamental plants like Mondo grass, Ligustrum, Peonies, and Siberian Iris.

We stopped at the Chongqing Art Institute on the zoo grounds. There were student artists under the tutelage of master artists in Chinese techniques, but there were also exhibits of masters' work in modern realism and expressionism. Very good work. The police inspected and approved of all exhibits to make sure they conformed to government standards. Currently they asked for objectionable art to be removed but no longer arrested the offending artists.

The weather was cool (10°C) and humid. In a couple months, the temperature would be 30-35°C and humid. Chongqing has been called the sweatbox of the Yangtze.

Lunch was in a downtown hotel. It was local Sichuan food but there was only one moderately spicy dish. I had been looking forward to spicy mopo tufu or twice cooked pork (huiguo rou) in their native habitat. I tried fried duck's head, which was ok. It was deep-fried and had a considerable amount of fine textured meat. I had eaten chicken and duck feet and fish heads in the past. Desert was fruit including large loquats (Eriobotrya japonica) and longans (Euphoria Longan) or dragon eyes.

Chongqing did not give the impression of a big city. People were not crowded and there was no heavy traffic. Downtown had almost no bicycles due to the hills. We saw some of the farm people with a long pole and ropes to carry almost anything anywhere for a few cents and vendors with slung baskets full of fruit and other produce. Several stick people were standing on the corners waiting to carry anything up the steep hills.

We were out to the airport in mid-afternoon for the flight to Xi'an. A two-hour flight landed at Changan airport about 50 miles from Xi'an. The bus took us straight to the hotel. We left about an hour later to attend dinner and a Tang Dynasty show.

Xi'an. Xi'an translates as "the western capitol". The city is encompassed on three sides by high, dry mountains that form a basin opening to the southeast. This basin collects and holds the smoke from numerous coal-fueled power plants and forms shadow reducing rainfall. There is dry land wheat farming and noodle manufacturing. The fields contained water catchments since this was a dry area. They were looking at wind generation with over 150 days wind annually funneled through the open pass.

Local habitation extends back 8,000 years. This area was a pottery center for at least that long. It was capital of the Western Zhou Dynasty (1066-221 BC). Emperor Qin Shi Huangdi defeated all his neighbors and unified all of China. He began a palace and created the terra cotta army to accompany him to the afterlife about 221 BC. The capitol city of Han Chan An was completed in 240 BC but destroyed 24 years later. The city was rebuilt about 499 AD in compliance with the fung schwei principles. During the Sui (581-618) and Tang (618-907) Dynasties the city grew to over a million. Present population in the area was about 21 million. Xi'an was near the eastern end of the Silk Road and the western end of the Great Wall.

In modern times the "Xi'an incident" took place in 1936. A local warlord kidnapped Chiang Kai-shek to force him to negotiate with the Communists. Zhou En Lai had arrived to negotiate.

On the way from the airport, we passed several mounds in the middle of the fields. These were tombs that had, hopefully, not been looted. This was dry land farming, orchards of apples and pears, and tree farms raising cottonwood and other broadleaf trees in a grand effort to reclaim the desert. There were also Ashoka trees. No birds.

Surprisingly in this land of drought there were half a dozen fish ponds that looked to be a quarter acre each. Three were dry and the other three had people fishing with poles in the cool afternoon.

On the way to the Tang Paradise dinner theatre, we passed through the old city wall. This is the third wall built about 600 years back of rammed earth. It is forty feet high, fifty feet thick and 15 miles long. This is the only complete city wall in China. It took eight years to construct 2,000 years ago and has recently taken thirty years to restore.

We passed the new soccer stadium. Traffic was jammed since the soccer game had just finished and the streets and freeway were running over with home-bound with traffic. Must be real fun jockeying a bus around.

Dinner was about ten courses of Tang style food and was very good. Cashew chicken and, separately, braised chicken. Next was a mushroom soup that tasted like French onion and had several kinds of mushrooms. Then a dozen more dishes. A slightly sweet Chinese Saki was served warm. I liked it better than Japanese Saki but was not overly impressed.

After dinner, we went up stairs to the theatre and enjoyed an outstanding show of music and dance dating from the Tang Dynasty. The show had music played on Tang instruments like Ruan (looked like a wooden banjo), Pipa (like a wooden ukulele), Jinghu (stringed stick mounted on a tin can), Guzheng (like a steel guitar), Gugin (flutes), drums, and gongs. Dances were flowing with swirling long silk sleeves. It would have been more interesting if I had not dozed off several times. I shot a lot of pictures anyway.

As we headed back to the hotel about 2100 there was a big ceremony at the city gate with dancers, music, and lots of lights. According to our guide, earlier in the day there had been a big ceremony – key to the city- for some dignitaries.

Tang Paradise Restaurant Tang Opera

The city had no new tall buildings. Construction was limited to eight floors for architectural compatibility with the ancient wall and historic structures and for earthquake safety. Many of the buildings and especially the roofs were in Mandarin style. The tallest old building is the Wild Goose Pagoda built by the early Buddhists.

Guzheng Player

Xian and City Wall

16 April 2006. Happy Easter. Breakfast was good. Regional differences: sweet tomato juice; flat tasting watermelon and cantaloupe (either not fully ripe or raised in drought conditions); real sweet rolls; good strawberries.

We had 30 minutes until the bus left, so Carol and some other women went shopping as soon as the shops opened.

Looking around the downtown area landscape plants included Chinese Juniper (<u>Juniperus</u> <u>chinensis</u>), Chinese Photinia (<u>Photinia</u> <u>villosa</u>), Chinese Cottonwood (<u>Populus</u> <u>Simonii</u>), palms (<u>Livingstona</u> <u>sp</u>.), Corkscrew Willow (<u>Salix</u> <u>matsudana</u>) and Camellia (<u>Camellia</u> <u>sinensis</u>). No birds. Not even sparrows.

On the road to the museum were fields and lots of young trees that could have been a windbreak or tree farm. Berry plants were growing in the fencerows and Camellia or tea plants were poking through the fence of someone's yard. Again, no birds.

The sun came out, and the mountains were visible. This was the first sun in several days.

The Qin Shi Huangdi Tomb complex consisted of two large building covering two of the eight excavation sites, a history museum and a gift shop/bookstore/restaurant. (Additional mounds containing Qin administrative personnel have been opened since our visit.)

The area was open and well landscaped with Chinese Juniper, Chinese Photinia, Chinese Cottonwood, and Corkscrew Willow. Their Crepe Myrtle (<u>Lagerstroemia</u> <u>speciosa</u>) was trimmed as badly as most American counterparts. I saw one bird, Eurasian Jay (<u>Garrulus</u> <u>glandarius</u>). I really wish I could have got out in the countryside away from ornamentals with a biologist to see the agriculture and the wild plants - the real China. I suppose I am lucky to have seen what I did.

The maybe ten acre plaza was paved with alternating paving blocks and perforated pavers planted with Bluegrass (?). Looked nice. This was broken into smaller areas with benches and some shade plants.

Anyway, we went through the first enclosure. It was about the size of six football fields. Not long ago, photography had been forbidden but it was allowed now. The scene was impressive. Rammed-earth walls 2.5 meters wide topped with burned log roof supports delineated pits where life-size soldiers and horses were arrayed in formation. There were relics of a brick wall and a well had been found. Many of the figures had been put back together and the cracks and missing sections replaced with epoxy.

The back two-thirds were test pits rather than excavation. There was a research area that was covered with piles of pieces that were being sorted. Each piece was cataloged and photographed. Along both sides were display signs in Chinese and English explaining various points of interest.

Reconstruction Area   Life-size Figures

Terracotta Army   Terracotta Overview

Research by today's craftsmen has identified the method of building the figures. Eight hundred artists and thousands of artist's helpers were brought in to create individual hands, heads and torsos. These were fired in the caves where they were cast. The parts were then assembled. Each warrior is an individual.

Local clay was used. The body and head were built by the coil method over several days to prevent cracking. This is then sculpted and the arms and legs were made in molds. The work was done in caves to stabilize the temperature and humidity. When the figures were dry they were baked in the same cave. The finished figures were painted. This process allowed about 700 figures a year to be finished over a ten year span. Each figure weighs about 700 pounds.

On one side of the hall were several large glass cases containing representative figures – a nobleman, an archer, a lancer. Each figure was life size and individual as to facial features and clothing details. (Facial recognition software was used on a group of 200 figures and determined each was different.) This army was supposed to support the Emperor in the afterlife. Wonder what happened to the soldier models?

Reconstructed Figure   Museum and Grounds

There was a peasant rebellion shortly after the Emperor died. Much of the roof over the figures was burned and collapsed damaging many of the figures.

The Emperor had also built a paradise garden with a map of the known world done in jade using mercury for water. They think it has been located in a mound nearby under 150 feet of rubble. Test wells have revealed mercury vapor but no test pits had been dug at this time. They have found two large step pyramids and a marble dome that may be the roof of the main tomb.

We went to the on-site restaurant for lunch followed by more shopping. It was interesting to watch the noodle maker.

Structure 2 was smaller and contained many artifacts including a reconstruction of one of two chariots that had been found.

The third museum covered much of Chinese history. On the way out we took another trip through the bookstore and watched the 360° movie screen showing 15 minutes of old style war.

The bus took us to the airport for the flight to Beijing. While we were waiting for the bus, I talked to our local guide about the vegetation.

She was the only guide that seemed to have much biological information on the whole trip. She identified several plants for me like twisted or Corkscrew Willow. I pointed out Chinese Photinia and some of the pandemic weed species like white clover (Trifolium repens) and Oxalis (Oxalis rubra?), which she wrote in her notebook.

We sat in the terminal waiting for the plane. All flights had been delayed because of bad weather near Beijing.

17April 2006. Humans had lived in the Beijing area for about 500,000 years. The first real settlement was about 1000 BC as a trading village on the Mongol and Korean border. By the Warring States Period (453-221 BC), the town was called Ji. In the Liao dynasty (916-1125), it was called Yanjing (Capital of Yan). Genghis Kahn destroyed the city in 1215 and rebuilt it as his capital, Dadu (Great Capital), also called Khanbaliq (Khan's city). In 1279, Kublai Khan made himself ruler of the largest empire in Old World history. A warlord named Zhu Yanchang captured the city in 1368 and it was renamed Beiping (Northern Peace). The Emperor Yongle renamed the city Beijing (Northern Capital) in the 1400's. Yongle also designed and built the Forbidden City and Tiantan and laid out the cities ring roads.

We were told we would have to reverse our tours for the day because a PRC friendly dignitary from Taiwan was in town, and the Great Wall was evacuated so he could have a secure visit. We went to the Ming Tombs first and the Wall after lunch.

Beijing Night Club   Beijing Traffic

A dust storm had blown through over night and, according to the morning paper, had dropped 300,000 tons of Gobi dust on everything. Cars, plants, streets, window ledges, anything outside were dusted with yellow brown dust.

Our bus flew along the freeway with a zillion cars plus trucks of live pigs and cattle and machinery. We came in through the Small Palace Gate and offloaded. The 13 actual tombs of the 16 Ming Emperors were about 3km north and we would not be seeing them.

Dust storm

Our entry was through the Lingxing Gate. We would be swimming up stream for over a half-mile along the Sacred Way towards the usual entrance through the Stone Arch and the Great Palace Gate. It made little difference since none of the gates are located in its exact historic location.

Sacred Way Figure   Sacred Way Animals

We passed the four obedient retainers, then the four civil servants, and then four military men. These marble statues were about 3 meters tall. Next came six pairs of animals with one of each pair resting and ready to take up the watch. First were horses, next were a pair of mythical beast (suanni), then elephants and camels, then another pair of beasts and, finally, a pair of lions.

Yellow dust covered everything. A workman was hosing the slippery dust off the center of the stone path.

Magpies (<u>Pica</u> <u>pica</u>) were feeding on the grounds beyond the statues. Cottonwood trees supported numerous magpie nests. The walk was lined on each side with a Privet (<u>Ligustrum</u> <u>vulgare</u>) hedge and a line of

Corkscrew Willow (<u>Salix</u> <u>matsudana</u>) backed up by a barrier of Chinese Juniper (<u>Juniperus</u> <u>chinensis</u>). Beyond this was a grove of Tenasserim Pine (<u>Pinus</u> <u>merkusii</u>).

Dahongmen   Gobi Dust

Beyond the lions was the Dahongmen (Great Red Gate) with three arches. The center gate was used only to carry the Emperor to his tomb. Through the center door sat a huge marble turtle (longevity symbol) with a 30-foot stele mounted on its back. Beyond this were a five-arched gate and the bus. Just remember that the Emperor's body and his wife would pass through the center door of the Dahongmen only when the Emperor died on the way to his tomb and that we came in the out.

Back on the highway, we rode several miles to the Superior Jade Factory for lunch and more shopping. It seemed a bit strange having a restaurant with a jade or pearl or rug factory, but it seemed to work. Lunch was nothing special, but they did have ice cream.

The carved jade in the entrance was massive and impressive. We were taken through the carving shop to see carvers at work. Then we were turned loose in the show room. My favorite pieces were several jade tea sets. They also had some of the best designs in pearl jewelry I had ever seen.

The Great Wall (Chángchéng) or 10,000 li wall stretches almost 3,000 miles from the Pacific Ocean near Korea and Shanhai Pass west to Jiayu Pass in the Gobi Desert at the end of the Silk Road. The original wall was started when Emperor Qin Shihuang (221-207 BC) defeated all the kingdoms and consolidated China for the first time. He connected all of the individual kingdom's walls into a single structure using hundreds of thousands of mostly prisoners as laborers over a ten-year period. Chi

Chi Kwan finished the wall in 575 at a cost of equivalent to a billion bucks. It never worked well as a defensive structure but was handy as an elevated highway joining Beijing to the Silk Road. Fifteen sentry towers using smoke and flag signals or runners could transmit messages relatively quickly. However, during the past 400 years the wall was abandoned and some sections almost disappeared. Tourist interest in the Wall in the 1950's was an incentive to rebuild parts of the Great Wall.

North Gate   Tower No. 8

We were driven 70 km north to the Badaling Great Wall. This section had been rebuilt and upgraded in 1957 including the addition of some handrails and a cable car. In 1990, the Great Wall Circle Vision Theatre was installed.

We climbed the steps to the North Gate and the top of the wall. I began walking NE towards North tower No.8 with hundreds of other people. Vendors were at the entrance and scattered along the wall selling hats and T-shirts. There were two men carving wall figures on small slabs of slate with a chisel and hammer and no eye protection.

Travel on the Wall was not easy. There were cobblestones, lots of steps and few handrails. The steps were varying thickness from 3" to nearly a foot that made hitting a rhythm in walking difficult. I passed the fort inside the wall and up to watchtower No. 7. I did not feel like climbing last set of 15° steps to get an official piece of paper saying I had climbed the Great Wall.

On Top of the Wall   Slope of the Wall

There were windows and firing ports scattered along the wall. The bottoms are parallel to the floor instead of being horizontal. Wonder how that impacted shooting. Huge drain spouts protruded from the wall to carry off storm water. Along about watchtower #4 was a public toilet. What did Genghis do before running water?

The hills inside the wall were terraced and steep trails lead to the ridgelines. Who knows how old this was. Plum blossoms were scattered across the hills. These trees looked like the almond trees of Greece.

Back at the entrance to the Wall, we gathered to wait for the bus. One of the big gift shops had a snack bar and bar. Lots of souvenirs: dollar ball caps, cheap T-shirts, jade(?) colored trinkets, Duvet sets stuffed with silk fibers, souvenir books. I inhaled two Chinese Cokes.

Chinese Coke   Vendor Stalls

We arrived back at the hotel in the late afternoon. It felt more like fall than April. We had a couple hours until we went out for dinner, but several people, including Carol, decided to go shopping. Carol found a

German restaurant and had schnitzel and came back in a pedicab. I had nap and a very good Beijing style supper with Tsingtao beer and a heavy, slightly sweet pinkish Chinese Saki.

I tried to call a student I knew from Beijing. Information told me that if I did not know her address and phone number or who she worked for that her number was restricted information. Why does information exist if everything is restricted? I guess it sounds better than "I can't find it". I found that there were 30 pages of people named Wong.

18 April 2006. The last full day of our trip dawned with a sun that looked like a pale full moon through the dust. We were scheduled to see Tiananmen Square, the Forbidden City, and the Summer Palace.

I asked for a Chinese breakfast and was told they had no such thing. Looking at the buffet line I found most of the makings for a traditional Chinese breakfast.

After breakfast, we loaded up and headed into the center of Beijing to see Tiananmen Square and the Forbidden City. We got off the bus near the Chinese National Museum across the street from Chairman Mao's Mausoleum and Tiananmen Square. It was cool and blustery and felt like south Texas winter. Glad we waited another week before coming to Beijing.

On the opposite side of the square was the Great Hall of the people. In the center was a tower, the Monument to the People's Heroes. We crossed the street into Tiananmen Square but did not visit any of the buildings. We were told not to photograph any activity by the police.

Tiananmen Square   Museum of the Revolution
Monument to Peoples Heroes

Tiananmen Square was originally constructed in 1651. In 1958, Mao quadrupled the size to 40.5 hectares (100 acres). Each of the rectangular flagstones was numbered and large enough to hold two people. Crowds in the square had exceeded one million people.

Thousands of people were standing in line around the Mausoleum for a glimpse of the Chairman. When Mao died, September 8, 1976, the Politburo decided on a two-week viewing period but changed this to perpetuity. A technique for permanent preservation was unknown at the time so a wax figure was made just in case. Both the real body and the wax figure were kept refrigerated below ground for security and one or the other was raised each day for viewing. It might take hours waiting in line to get in for a short peek. Entrance was free but many people bought flowers to place on the tomb. There was a joke that the flowers were picked up and resold in the Capitalist manner and Mao would roll over if he knew what was happening. Memorabilia such as key rings, mugs, and T-shirts was on sale in the square. We bought a cheap Mao wristwatch.

The Great Hall of the People was on the west side of the square. It is 310m (1017 ft) long. It is where the congress sits. It contains a hall that can seat 10,000 people or serve dinner to 5,000. It was completed in ten months in 1958-59.

On the east side of the square were the Museum of Chinese History and the Museum of the Chinese Revolution.

In the center of the square stands the monument to the People's Heroes, a 36m (118 ft) obelisk of red Quindao granite. It was completed by May Day, 1958, and had bas-relief scenes of historic events.

Flag Pole   Mao Mausoleum

On the north end of the square was the tallest flagpole in China. A huge flag was raised at sunrise and lowered at sunset with thousands of people observing the precision military performance. No flag in all China is allowed to be higher.

There were thousands of people in the square as individuals but mostly as groups of school kids in uniforms, veterans, ethnic groups in traditional dress, and families. We made our way to the northeast corner of the square to a pedestrian underpass to the Forbidden City.

Entry was through the Tiananmen Gate into the passage between the walls of the Working People's Cultural Palace and Zhongshan Park then passed through the Meridian Gate formerly used only by the Emperor's official visitors and into the Forbidden City. Zhongshan Park was designed in 1421 for the imperial family. It contains lawns and gardens and an amphitheatre, teahouse and pond. We did not see this or the gardens in the People's Cultural Park.

Entrance to Imperial Palace   Crowd

The Imperial Palace complex, also called the Forbidden City (Zijin Cheng), is an architectural masterpiece and one of the greatest construction feats in history. The site was chosen and construction began by the Mongol Yuan dynasty (1279-1368) and completed by the Ming Emperor Yong Le (also known as Yongle) using thousands of workers and artisans. It was sacked and looted by the Manchu army in 1644 but restored and enlarged by the Qing (Ching) Dynasty. The complex covered 101.2 hectares (250 acres) and was surrounded by a moat and protected by a 10.7m (35 ft) wall. There were six main palaces and many smaller buildings containing over 9,000 rooms.

The Palace grounds were divided into two sections. The foreground contained three large public halls where Ming and Qing emperors conducted state business.

The rear section contained three main palaces, several smaller palaces, and the Imperial Garden. From here, 24 "Son's of Heaven" had ruled from the Dragon Throne.

The Palace was looted in 1911 during the rebellion that overthrew the Qing dynasty. The Japanese took more loot from the complex during the 1930's. Chang Kai-shek "rescued" and sent boatloads of art and treasure to Taiwan in 1949 when he and the KMT retreated. The PRC opened the Palace as a public park in 1949.

Imperial Throne   Lion Outside Palace

We passed through the Meridian Gate (Wumen) into the foreground and across the marble bridge over the Golden Water Stream (Jinshui He). We went to the Gate of Supreme Harmony (Taihemen) braced by two huge bronze lions and entered a huge courtyard capable of holding 90,000 people. (My old friend Julian Kung was there as a student at Beijing University. There is a picture of him sitting on one of the great bronze lions.)

Next in order was the Hall of Perfect Harmony (Zhonghedian). Built in 1420, this served as a dressing room where the Emperor would put on his formal robes. It was also where foreigners were greeted, the next year's seeds were blessed, and other similar ceremonies. Exiting the hall, stairs bracket the dragon pavement carved from a single 200-ton block of marble. Leaving the plaza, we passed a four-star restroom, which I had to inspect. I must say, the local backwoods gas station has nothing to worry about.

Through the Gate of Heavenly Purity (Tianqingmen), we entered the Palace of Heavenly Purity (Tianqinggong) where the Dragon Throne was located with other symbols of office. This also contained the king's five bedrooms (he never slept in the same place twice). He had a different concubine rolled up in a rug every night brought to his bed of the night by eunuchs. Every girl child in the country was subject to selection for the Emperor's harem. If she did not make the grade she could get married and on with her life.

Next, was the Hall of Union (Jiaotaidian). It contained the clepsydra (a 2500-year-old water clock) and a mechanical clock built in 1797.

The final palace was the Palace of Earthly Tranquility (Kunninggong) where the Ming empresses lived. To either side were the East and West Palaces, used as libraries and quarters for the umpteen concubines.

We went through the Imperial Garden (Yuhuayuan) and exited through the Chengguangen and the Shunzhenmen gates and across the moat. It was about a half-mile along the moat to the bus. It was still cool and blustery, but the cherry blossoms and irises were in bloom.

So far on this trip, everything had gone well, but I had enjoyed about as much of this as I could stand.

The bus took us to a restaurant (that just happened to be co-located with a pearl factory) for lunch and more shopping before the last stop – the Summer Palace.

The Summer Palace (Yiheyuan) grounds cover 280 hectares (692 acres) 11km NW of Tiananmen Square. The present structure was actually the third summer residence. The first was built in the 12th century and burned by French and British troops in 1860. The Dowager Empress Ci Xi built the next palace in 1888 using funds intended to train the imperial Navy (on the lake?). This one was destroyed by British troops during the Boxer Rebellion in 1900. The third one was built in 1903. The Empress built Kunming Lake to train the Navy then used more funds to build the famous marble boat.

It was windy and misty. We entered through a big red gate and by several buildings and gardens including the bedroom of the Empress. We passed through another gate and through the Hall of Benevolence and Longevity (Leshantang) out onto the lakefront. We walked the 700m Long Corridor (supposed to be the longest covered walkway) originally painted with murals of mythical creatures. The Red Guard whitewashed this. There was a lot of construction and renovation going on, and we bypassed the man-made Longevity Hill. At the end of the walk sat the marble boat. We were lucky enough to get a boat ride back across the lake and then walk over the 17-arch bridge to the exit. This park was popular and relatively crowded for a weekday.

On the way out, a boy and girl about five said, "Hello". I replied, "Hello, how are you?" They said, "Fine". I asked their names in Mandarin. They grinned and their mother told them to tell me their names. The little girl said, "Jasmine" and hid behind her mother. The little boy grinned and said, "Tarzan" and ran off to play with his friends.

Entrance to Summer Palace

Marble Boat

Kunming Lake

17 Arch Bridges

We returned to the hotel and got ready for our last Chinese meal of the trip, Peking Duck. The meal had a dozen or so dishes including the duck rolled in flat bread with cucumbers and plum jam. They served Ji beer (the original name of Beijing) and a sweet fruity Saki.

19 April 2006. We were up early and tried to get everything packed so nothing would be damaged. After breakfast, we went out to buy another suitcase. We also bought a Mao watch and a couple T-shirts. Our bags were in the hall for pick up by 1100. Then we went out for a burger. Two burgers and drinks ran over $30.

Downtown Beijing   Local Mall

We were on the plane about 1600. Above the clouds our route was more to the northeast across the Primorye environmental region: near Fushun and Jilin in Chinese Manchuria; over the Amur River north of Lake Khanka, the largest lake in the region; over Russian Khrebet Sikhotr Alin and across the Tartarskiy Provolis to Sakhalin Island; over the Sea of Okhotsk and the Kamchatka Peninsula to the Bering Sea. This area is home to many endangered species including the Amur tiger and leopard, fish owl, raccoon dog, Sakhalin deer, musk deer, and the Siberian black bear. Mandarin and other ducks were returning and the ice was breaking up.

We were feet dry over Alaska's Nunuvak Island and the Yukon Delta. Continuing up the Yukon River we entered Canada crossing the Yukon, Northwest Territory, northern Alberta and Saskatchewan, and Manitoba. We turned south NE of Winnipeg. We landed in Chicago an hour later than we took off on the same day after 14 flying hours.

20 April 2006. We were in San Antonio a little after lunch. Where to next?

After Thoughts

After having wanted to see China for a half century the trip lived up to many of my expectations. I know that trying to see that much in two weeks presents logistic problems and a lot of decision making on where to go and what to see and how to satisfy most of the members of a diverse group. There are all sorts of specialized tours but this Viking tour did a good job of juggling resources and time.

One thing I would have liked is a guide more knowledgeable in natural resources like birds and plants. For this I need another specialized tour. The young lady guide in Xi'an knew some of the plants and I identified some for her.

Other side trips I would like include the Jewish community in Shanghai and any hutongs left in Hong Kong and Beijing and the former bomb shelters in Beijing. These and other features are disappearing replaced by condos and malls. The Flying Tiger museum in Chongqing is another footnote to recent history disappearing under the march of progress.

Could not complain about the weather. Weather is always a variable and one of the aspects of making the trip memorable. Hong Kong and Shanghai skyscrapers disappearing into the fog. Shifting shades of green, sun, and shade on the Li River. Xian's historic smog. Goby Desert dust storms dusting Beijing. I was really impressed with flying over the pole and seeing the ice fields, Siberia, and the Goby Desert.

I added 24 new birds to my list plus a number of plants. This is always variable depending on location, weather, and time of year. I am well satisfied.

Hotels were all five star. Food was outstanding. I got my Chinese breakfast in spite of the hotels claim to be modern and up to date. One complaint of sorts was the lack of Sichuan cooking in the heart of Sichuan. To eat Mao's favorite dish - stuffed tofu – in Mao's home territory would have been exciting.

Various discussions brought up facts and opinions. One frank discussion I forgot to mention was talking about racial epithets. American soldiers called Orientals "slopes" and "flat face". Orientals called westerners "big nose" and "round eye". I asked about the term "kui lo" (foreign devil) and was told hesitantly that it was an old term and they did not use this term because it was considered officially derogatory. All these terms and a lot more are derogatory and, we agreed, should not be used.

One thing I learned was that the Chinese are generally not bitter about Mao and the Red Guard. They are ambivalent about whether Mao was an oppressor or liberator, educator or autocrat. Mao sent the teachers to work the farms and factories but adopted the Western typewriter and the pinyin format as the partial replacement for Chinese pictographs. He renamed everyplace using their historic name and spelling the names using pinyin. He was responsible for mass education but at a lower level, a modern building program and pushing China into the 20th century. He rewrote newspapers and books in English style reading left to right but alienated the older generation who read right to left

China began to westernize with the help of the Russians and has continued with assistance from Japanese and Americans. Education. Business. Industry. Engineering. Everything was modernizing. The Olympics in 2008. Clean Beijing and other cities. I would suggest that the best time ever to visit China would be in 2009 when the Olympic dust has settled but the country is still clean.

Birds

Hong Kong and Kowloon
Spotted Doves (<u>Streptopelia</u> <u>chinensis</u>),
Brown Shrike (<u>Lanius</u> <u>cristatus</u>),
Red-Whiskered Bulbul (<u>Pycnonotus</u> <u>jocosus</u>)
Eurasian Tree Sparrow (<u>Passer</u> <u>montanus</u>).

Victoria peak
Red-Whiskered Bulbuls (<u>Pycnonotus</u> <u>jocosus</u>
Eastern Marsh-Harriers (<u>Circus</u> <u>spilonotus</u>)

Repulse Bay
Red-Whiskered Bulbuls (<u>Pycnonotus</u> <u>jocosus</u>)
Crested Mynas (<u>Acridotheres</u> <u>cristatellus</u>

Aberdeen
Black Kite (<u>Milvus</u> <u>migrans</u>)

Guilin and
Large-billed Crow (<u>Corvus</u> <u>macrorhynchus</u>)

Li River
Black-crowned Night-heron (<u>Nycticorax</u> <u>nycticorax</u>)
Eurasian Tree Sparrow (<u>Passer</u> <u>montanus</u>).
Great Cormorants (<u>Phalacrocorax</u> <u>carbo</u>)
Eastern Marsh Harrier (<u>Circus</u> <u>aeruginousus</u>)
White-crowned Forktail (<u>Enicurus</u> <u>leschenaultia</u>)

Wushan
Barn Swallow (<u>Hirundo</u> <u>rustica</u>)

Lesser Three Gorges
Plumbeous Redstart (<u>Rhyacornis</u> <u>fuliginosus</u>)
Barn Swallow (<u>Hirundo</u> <u>rustica</u>)
Green-Billed Malkoha (<u>Phaenicophaeus</u> <u>tristis</u>)

Fengdu
Bronzed Drongos (<u>Dicrurus</u> <u>aeneus</u>)
Common Black-Headed Gull (<u>Larus</u> <u>ridibundus</u>)

Chongqing

River Little Egret (<u>Egretta</u> <u>garzetta</u>)
Herring Gull (<u>Larus</u> <u>argentatus</u>)
Barn Swallow (<u>Hirundo</u> <u>rustica</u>)

Park   Black-crowned Night-heron (<u>Nycticorax</u>
                        <u>nycticorax</u>)
                        Little Egret (<u>Egretta</u> <u>garzetta</u>)
                        Azure-winged Magpie (<u>Cyanopica</u> <u>cyanus</u>)
                        Common Blackbird (<u>Turdus</u> <u>merula</u>)
                        Eye-browed Thrush (<u>Turdus</u> <u>obscurus</u>)

Xi'an   Eurasian Jay (<u>Garrulus</u> <u>glandarius</u>)

Beijing   Black-billed Magpie (<u>Pica</u> <u>pica</u>)

Plants

Kowloon

Lettuce Tree (<u>Pisonia</u> <u>alba</u>)
Flamboyant or Royal Poinciana (<u>Delonix</u> <u>regia</u>)
Bottlebrush (<u>Callistemon</u> <u>lanceolatus</u>)
Australian Pine (<u>Auracaria</u> <u>heterophylla</u>)
Geiger Tree (<u>Cordia</u> <u>sebestena</u>)
African Tulip Tree (<u>Spatheodea</u> <u>campanulata</u>)
Hong Kong Orchid Tree (<u>Bauhinia</u> <u>purpurea</u>)
Fiddlewood (<u>Citharexylum</u> <u>spinosum</u>)
Ixoria (<u>Ixoria spp.</u>)
Lantana (<u>Lantana sp.</u>)
Plumbago (<u>Plumbago</u> <u>sp.</u>)
Banana (<u>Musa</u> <u>spp.</u>)
Oleander (<u>Nerium</u> <u>spp.</u>)
Crepe Myrtle (<u>Lagerstroemia</u> <u>speciosa</u>)
Manila palms (<u>Veitchia</u> <u>merrillii</u>)
Fish tail Palms (<u>Caryota</u> <u>mitis</u>)
Madagascar Palm (<u>Chrysalidocarpus</u> <u>lutescens</u>)
Hurricane Palm (<u>Ptychosperma</u> <u>macarthurii</u>)
Chinese Fan Palm (<u>Livistona</u> <u>chinensis</u>)

Victoria Peak

Wild cane
Indian Laurel (<u>Calophyllum</u> <u>inophyllum</u>)
White clover (<u>Trifolium</u> <u>repens</u>)
Purple Oxalis (<u>Oxalis</u> <u>rubra</u>?)
Crepe Myrtle (<u>Lagerstroemia</u> <u>speciosa</u>)
Yellow Oxalis (<u>Oxalis</u> sp.)
White lantana (<u>Lantana</u> sp.)
Several small composites.

Guilin

Osmanthus (<u>Osmanthus</u> <u>aurantiacus</u>)
Osmanthus (<u>O. fragrans</u>)
Bamboo (<u>Bambusa</u> <u>vulgaris</u>)
Ashoka or Mast Trees (<u>Polyalthia</u> <u>longifolia</u>)
Wild plums (<u>Prunus</u> <u>tenella</u>)
Henna (<u>Lawsonia</u> <u>inermis</u>)

Cedars (<u>Toona</u> <u>sinensis</u>)
Pine (<u>Pinus</u> <u>Massoniana</u>)
Park landscape plants included Rhododendrons, Cannas, Siberian Iris and Creeping Charlie

Shanghai   **Yuyuan Garden.**
Weeds included <u>Draba</u>, <u>Brassica</u>, and <u>Plantago</u>.
Ferns and mosses grew on the roof tiles.
Cherry trees (<u>Prunus</u> <u>serrulata</u>)
Japanese maple (<u>Acer</u> <u>palmatum</u>)
Cedars
Pines
Crepe Myrtle (<u>Lagerstroemia</u> <u>speciosa</u>)
Wisteria (<u>Wisteria</u> <u>sp</u>.)
Weeping Willow (<u>Salix</u> <u>sp</u>.)

Xiling Gorge   Osmanthus (<u>Osmanthus</u> <u>aurantiacus</u>)
Spirea (<u>Spirea</u> <u>arborea</u>)

Wu Gorge   Osmanthus (<u>Osmanthus</u> <u>aurantiacus</u>)
Henna (<u>Lawsonia</u> <u>inermis</u>)
Wild Plum (<u>Prunus</u> <u>tenella</u>)
Spirea (<u>Spirea</u> <u>arborea</u>)

Lesser Three Gorges   Rubus (<u>Rubus</u> <u>palmatus</u>)
<u>Geranium</u> sp
Spirea (<u>Spirea</u> <u>arborea</u>)

Snow Cave   Ligustrum (<u>Ligustrum</u> <u>sinensis</u>)
Mulberry (<u>Morus</u> <u>multicaulis</u>)
Philippine Violet (<u>Barleria</u> <u>cristata</u>)
Grape fern (<u>Botrychium</u> <u>sp</u>)
Mosses
Liverworts

Chongqing Zoo   <u>Ranunculus</u> sp.
<u>Sisymbrium</u> sp

Eupatorium sp
Veronia sp
Geranium sp
Siberian Iris
Bidens sp
Sonchus sp.

Xian
Tenasserim Pine (Pinus merkusii)
Ashoka or Mast Tree (Polyalthia longifolia)
Chinese Photinia (Photinia villosa)
Day Jasmine (Cestrum diurnum)
Berry plants in the fencerows
Camellia (Camellia sinensis) or tea plants
Chinese Juniper (Juniperus chinensis)
Cottonwood (Populus Simonii)
Palms (Livingstona sp.)
Corkscrew Willow (Salix matsudana)
White clover (Trifolium repens)
Oxalis (Oxalis rubra?)
Crepe Myrtle (Lagerstroemia speciosa)

Beijing
Wild plum (Prunus tenella)
Corkscrew Willow (Salix matsudana)
Chinese Juniper (Juniperus chinensis)
Privet (Ligustrum vulgare)

Other

Green dragon fly
Butterflies that looked like cabbage butterflies
red panda (Ailurus fulgens)   Chongqing Zoo
giant panda (Ailuropoda melanoleuca)   Chongqing Zoo

These poems were composed during a trip to China, April 2006.

Flying to Siberia
Hong Kong Growing
Nathan Road 2006
Kowloon City Park 2006
Inside a Zen Painting
Shanghai Fog
Shanghai Pages
Xi'an
Beijing – History of a Name

Additional poems in the Chinese style

Arriving in Hong Kong
The White Bat
Tea Renku
Long March Tea House
Dim Sum
Demise of the Monkey, Night of no Moon
Polluted Night Renku
Hong Kong Chestnuts, 1978
Nathan Road 2006
Cat Street, Hong Kong

Flying to Siberia
A Lesson in Geography

Times change.
Fifty years ago this flight path
would have encountered
missiles and interceptor wrath.

Across the top of the world finds
white ice of the Arctic Ocean with
long blue/black leads and pressure ridges
from the sea in motion

East across the Siberian Sea.
South of Ostrov Novaya Sabir lay
ice dirty brown from Gobi Desert dust
sucking up sunlight.

Landfall between the Rivers Indigirka and Yana
then west to the Lena R. delta.
South up the Lena Valley
Over tundra and taiga.

Taiga miles - stunted conifers cut by long straight roads
strip mines and clear-cut timber stands.

Docks and loading areas on the Lena and
a tug and barges breaking the ice.

Tundra -
scattered aspen and conifers
a million huttogs (prairie potholes).

Over flying Zhigansk,
in the state of Sakha in Russia.
Trans-Siberian Railroad tracks disappear east and west.
Rough mountains of the Yablonovy Khrebet.
Lake Baykal.

111

Ulan Ude in the Buryatia in Russian Mongolia.
Over the Hentuyn Nuruu Mountains.
Ulaanbaatar, Mongolia.

The Gobi Desert -
flat with a few huttogs.
A railroad running north/south.
Sand from light tan to a darker brown.

Into China
West of Xian
under clouds.

carl4Apr0306

Hong Kong Growing

Twenty-five years ago
Hong Kong had tall buildings
And garishly lighted streets and signs.
Rolls Royce taxis.
Double decked busses.
Narrow streets.
Hutongs like Cat Street.
Outdoor fish and bird markets.
Street of the Thousand-Year Egg.
Shops with gold statues and armed guards.

This time buildings were more numerous and taller
based on feng shui for good luck.
Night-time buildings colored and even animated.
Streets crowded with taxis and busses.
Subways new and busy.
Streets run one-way only.
Hutongs long destroyed.
New museums, theatres, and schools.

Good? Bad?
Different.

Nathan Road 2006

Twenty-five years ago at 0800
I was the only one on Nathan Road
But the bingo man and the chestnut vendor

Today Nathan Road has changed.
At 0800 the street was full of people,
Indians and Muslims rushing to work,
cars and cabs and busses rushing.
I was certainly not alone now.

carl4Apr0506

Kowloon City Park 2006

When I first saw the park in 1979
it was grass and trees
neatly trimmed grass
old folks doing Tai Chi

In April 2006
the park had a large mosque
and shopping malls
no grass to trim
no Tai Chi.
Progress or just change?

carl4Apr0506

Inside a Zen Painting

Floating on the Li River
More real than a Zen painting
Rounded karst mountains
Three hundred millions old
Shades of green transforming,
Shifting shades of green
Clouds and sunlight changing values
Fog rising and falling
Fog advancing and retreating
Mountains appearing and disappearing
Splashes of yellow and white and plum
Quiet river
Ancient farms
Ducks, cormorants, and water buffalo
Giant bamboos
Ancient caves
Thick silent sounds of the river

                                        carlApr0806

Shanghai Fog

Shanghai fog was cool and wet
and glowed pink and blue and green.
Stumps of buildings
left you to wonder
what was in the cloud
unseen.

CarlApr0906

Shanghai Pages

Like thumbing the pages of a thick book
Modern skyscrapers pierce the clouds
today, waiting for tomorrow.
Rapidly flipping a page
to square blocky Russian and Red Guard style
Bombing and fire of Japanese pages with footnote
50,000 Austrian Jews escaping Hitler's fire
but jumping into a Japanese pan.

More pages
Mandates, revolution, rebellion, coercion
Qing and Qin;
Shang and Tang
Mongols and madmen
Visible inside the page
If not on the surface
Interesting reading.

CarlApr0906

Xi'an

The end of the Silk Road
The start of the Great Wall
The center of nowhere
But having it all

The western capitol
United the world
Destroyer of culture
But one flag unfurled

Unstable Emperor
Qin Shi Huangdi
Conquered all his neighbors
But he was mad as he could be

He commissioned a life-size army
Made from terracotta clay
Men and horses to protect him
In the afterlife some day

His army still lies waiting
Buried by the desert sand
And the Emperor?
He is dead 2,000 years
Just another mortal man.

CarlApr1106

Beijing –History of a Name

Beijing, capital of China
A trading post 3,000 years past
On the Mongol border with Korea
Called Ji but this did not last

A thousand years ago it was called Yanjing
The capital of the Yan
In 1215 it was destroyed and rebuilt as Khanbalig
A capital for Genghis Kahn

Zhu Yanchang took the city in 1368
Naming it Northern Peace (in Chinese, Beiping)
Five hundred years ago Emperor Yongle
Called it his northern capitol by today's name, Beijing

carlApr1506

Arriving in Hong Kong

The interminable western Pacific night
finally punctured by a yellow spec
then more
by Macao,
Hong Kong
and the coastal island lights

The yellow glow
of low voltage and low wattage lights
differs from the stark white
or the peach colored halogen lights
of the Western world.

More lights appear as we begin
the approach to Kai Tak airport
diving into a mass of fireflies.
Diving
Diving.
Then ships' masts begin zipping past
and I look into a living room with the TV on
just before we gently tough contested earth.

Carl/790501/Arriving

The White Bat

Plums had set on the old gnarled tree
when a hoary white bat found us,
circled us
and gave us a thousand years.

Many plums have ripened.
Our time is held in
a polished ironwood box
carved with a peach.
Bats on the four corners.
The box rests on a table
between our chairs.

Take my hand.
I will keep you as warm
as our old kung
until the owl cries in the night.

TEA Renku

Unfortunate man.
In such a hurry that he
will drink first steep tea.
While the kettle boils and steams
Time to rest, relax, reflect.

Kung fu cha is strong.
Made outside on open fire,
Heady odor wafts.
Tea jar, teapot, all I need.
Art, utility, company.

Sun sinking, sky orange.
Martins sing chee cha chee chee
Water boils for us
Teahouse on a pond, frogs sing
Warm fire, sounds of night, old friends.

Thunder in the night.
Mist swirls as morning birds wake
Hot tea and yogurt
Tai che in the still wet grass
Sun and hours of toil til dusk.

carl/920306

Long March Tea House

Seventy years back
the Kuo Ming Tang
chased Mao on his Long March

Early morning in a small village in Schezuan
several KMT soldiers
came into a mountain tea house
on a cold, cold morning.

They warily eyed the other customers
in the small dark building in the mountains
and drank from house cups.
Some other customers had their own cups
and looked like woodcutters and farmers.

They spoke different dialects in their groups.
finishing tea and hands warm they all
bowed to each other and exited the tea house
each group in a different direction.
Each group quickly disappeared into the woods.

An hour later the shooting began again.

carl 15 Aug o4

DIM SUM

Dim Sum means "light snack" usually
Accompanied by Yum Cha (tea) and talk.
At the Sam Pan Garden Dim Sum
Begin with shrimp dumpling (Har Gau)
Spareribs (Pai Kwat)
Black dragon tea

Steamed dumpling with a thousand year egg (Cha Siu Bau)
Chrysanthemum buns with many fillings
Adventurous dishes like steamed duck feet
Steamer baskets with wondrous smells
Jasmine tea.

Glutinous congees with raw fish or taro
Salted Ba-Jen congee with sea cucumbers
Indian tea

Deserts like La Ba, congee of fruit
Mi Kao, the sweet rice cakes
Ba Bao rice

Fried bananas with honey
Dragon eyes
Rare white tea

Dim Sum
Dim Sum
Dim Sum

Carl/9804

Demise of the Monkey, Night of no Moon

The golden sun-orb
descends deliberately
towards a lucky red horizon
on a clear, cool evening.
No moon precedes or follows the sun
pursued by the Eastern dragon of night.

So dies the Year of the Monkey
and begins a night of no moon.

The dawn breaks red,
then orange.
the mother hen sun
with the moon under its wing
cracks the vault of heaven.

With a faint "ert, ert" of a young cock
the Year of the Rooster begins.

Auspicious signs for the new year.

carl 4649/01/01 (93/01/22)

Polluted Night Renku

The moon on high is
a white silver disc set in jet.
The moon is red brass
when air pollution stings
my eyes
and irritates my lungs.

carl

Hong Kong Chestnuts, 1978

A walk down Nathan Street at dawn is a private walk
with my wife and son past Kowloon Park.
No one is in sight except a chestnut vendor a block away
warming his hands as chestnuts begin to roast.
No one else is out in the cool white dawn.

The chestnut man eyes us warily
and greets us in English with a Shanghai accent.
I show off and reply in Mandarin and warm my hands.
Then I purchase a bag of hot chestnuts
and put one hot nut in each of my son's jacket pockets.
The old man grins and wishes us well.

Carl980404

Cat Street, Hong Kong

Just off Hollywood Road in Hong Kong
was Cat Street where, shoulder to shoulder,
we wandered the flea market
My son spotted a bright red jacket
which he wanted.
The old woman handed him a blue one
but my son insisted on the red.
In broken English she explained the red
was the color for girl children
She would not sell a red jacket to a boy
and allow him to be subject to ridicule.
In a world of the poor, a principled merchant.
Carl 78

Ηελσινκι το Στ. Πετερσβυργ
το Μοσχοω

(Helsinki to St. Petersburg
to Moscow)

June 2010
Carl Lahser

Helsinki to St. Petersburg to Moscow
June 2010

This year's trip was north to Finland and Russia on a Viking Cruise. On 18 Jun we flew to Helsinki for three days. On 22 Jun we went to St. Petersburg. After four days in St Petersburg we sailed the MV Viking Surkove for a five day trip up the Neva and Volga rivers to Moscow with stops in Mandrogy, Kizhi, Goritzy, Yarosiavi and Uglich. We spent 3+ days in Moscow and flew out of Moscow Domodedovo on July 4 to Dulles and San Antonio. The trip was unique in that the route roughly followed the southern edge of the taiga or boreal forest. It was ecologically interesting.

I have met several people who had been to Russia or at least Moscow over the past twenty years and their comments were pretty much noncommittal other than Russia has probably changed. But no details. This reminds me of Huck Finn and his experience with the medicine show play where half the town showed up one night and the other half the following night. On the third night everyone in town showed up with a lynching rope but the actors' had skipped town.

I checked the CDC and no additional shots are required. Measles, mumps and chickenpox, swine flu and malaria are present in both Finland and Russia but presented no problem.

Historical temperature ranges for this time frame are from the upper 40s to maybe 80. Russian labor laws limit the work day to 7 hours if the temperature exceeds 28.5°C (83°F) and only one hour if the temperature reaches 32.5°C (90.5°F). I guess this is due to no air conditioning. (Shortly after we returned there were reports of the Baltic water temperature rising to 20°C with a blanket of bluegreen alga. Moscow had heavy smog from peat fires and forest fires and temperatures had hit 38°C exceeding the record of 37°in 1928.)

A jacket was necessary on some occasions. Late June and July are historically warm and dry but a jacket and an umbrella good to have.

There was no Icelandic volcanic ash to contend with. The air routes had shifted to north of Iceland. South of Iceland there was volcanic ash from the Eyjafjallajükull volcano eruption to contend with. Ice covered or glaciovolcanoes. Heat from the eruption instantly melting and boiling the covering ice. Magma hitting the steam instantly exploding into tiny fragments creating ash clouds.

I looked on Google and other search engines for information on plants, butterflies, birds, seashells, etc., without much luck. I only took a book on northern European birds and one on flowers and I bought a book on European Insects in Finnish with pictures and English names. The trip covered the peak for spring wild flowers. Finland and northern Russia looked similar to southern Canada with mixed trees and wet meadows. I identified common plants and birds with my best guess.

Non-rechargeable batteries went on this trip. The rechargeables only stand 8-10 recharges and take 4-8 hours to recharge so I have had to dispose of many of the rechargeable batteries used on previous trips. I took a GPS, UV light, two digital cameras, two digital mini-recorders and a new notebook computer.

There were several comprehensive food guides and guides to entertainment on the Internet but I have found these trips don't leave much to the traveler discretion. The tours were general interest and included history and art and the impacts of 400 years of war. This was not a specialized tour.

18 Jun 2010. Friday. We were up about 0600 and ready for the taxi by 0830. It only took a half hour for check in and security.

United took off from San Antonio on time. Our steed was a CRJ 700 (Canadian Regional Jet). This is a short people's plane with four seats wide with a narrow center aisle designed for short trips. It was cloudy but smooth until we approached Chicago O'Hare. We landed and began looking for SAS (Air Sweden) at terminal 5. This required going through customs and security again and rechecking baggage at the international terminal.

There was a big black cloud to the SW of O'Hare with lightning. After boarding an Airbus A319 we sat on the plane on the taxiway for about two hours in a lightning storm.

There were half a dozen screaming kids taking turns annoying everyone. Take off was two hours late. The screamers finally quieted down after we took off.

Our route was north to Milwaukee then east across Lake Michigan to about Shelby, MI. We turned north to Sauté St. Marie, across Canada to Timmons, Ontario, then NE just south of James Bay. We crossed Quebec and Labrador to about Goose Bay in the setting sun.

Snow still covered much of the forest. Sunset was red orange masterpiece. It was twilight until the sun came over the eastern horizon about two hours later. There was open water off of Labrador for a few minutes then we were over pack ice all the way to Greenland. We crossed southern Greenland along the Arctic Circle. There were clear areas over both coasts showing less snow cover than on past trips.

Greenland

The course went north of Iceland instead of a hundred miles south as before the volcano. We were over a cloud deck until we were feet dry near Bergen, Norway. The clouds continued as we crossed north of Oslo and landed in Stockholm on the east coast of Sweden two hours late.

19 Jun. Saturday. SAS rescheduled us on another plane and said to go to gate F33. Half a mile later the people at the gate said we would have to go to the SAS service center "down that way". About a mile and several stops for directions like "We think it is down that way." we finally found the unmarked Service Center and got our new tickets and boarding passes. Back to gate F33. At least SAS gave us food vouchers for their booboo.

Aralanda airport was several miles from town and surrounded by woods. I saw several crows near the runway strutting along snagging bugs.

The interior of the airport reminded me of strip malls with most of the shops empty. The architecture looked about 30 years old. There were few passengers I guess because it was a Saturday.

We arrived at the Helsinki airport (about 60°N) and went through customs and immigration. Out in the lobby we expected to find our ride to the hotel. No Viking driver. We took a taxi to our hotel the Radisson Blu for 30 Euros (€).

The trip into town passed through what looked similar to New England with mixed industrial areas and bedroom communities. Streets and freeways were modern and adequate for a city of 600,000. Houses and businesses and warehouses. Streets were lined with Linden (Tilia cordata), Horse Chestnut (Aesculus hippocastanum), London Plane trees (Platanus hybrida) and Mountain Ash or Rowan (Sorbus aucuparia). Introduced lavender Lilacs (Syringia vulgaris) and red-purple rhododendron (Rhododendron ponticum) dotted the landscape. Temperature was 48°F and overcast.

We checked in and found the Viking representative. I asked about reimbursement of the taxi. First she asked why we had not called if we were going to be late and then said we would have to wait until we were on the ship. (The ship said wait til I got home. I called Viking and they agreed to the refund. No money but $250 credit on our next cruise.)

Then she said the train tracks were being repaired so no train to St Petersburg. I asked about van or bus and she said the roads were not safe (?) so we would fly on a Russian commuter airline. Safe? We made reservations for a couple tours around Helsinki.

The renovated hotel dated back to the 1920s. The room was decorated in Swedish Modern. The bed was at a diagonal with a dressing table was in the corner behind a stained glass headboard. The closet was circular with stained glass panels. The mirrors were art deco. The bed was covered

20 Jun. Sunday. About 0900 we started on a cool overcast walking tour of downtown. Across the old market square (Rautatientori Jornvagstorger). It was paved with granite blocks. Most of the buildings were built from granite blocks to prevent fires from periodic invasions.

On the east side were a couple of casinos and restaurants including the Texas Bar with a big green saguaro cactus. On the south was the national art museum. On the north side was a Mexican and a Nepalese restaurant and an office building. We crossed the square to the Empire style railroad station that looked like it belonged in a Batman movie. Through the railroad station lined with shops to the Soma Building. Past the modern art museum's modern building. Along Mannerheimintie past several statues to the Swedish Theatre.

Train Station

I tried the GPS. Four satellites eventually locked on but no location.

We walked along the north side of the esplanade (Pohjoisesplandei) lined with Linden trees. Many of the buildings dated to the 1920 with art deco details above the doors and windows. Most of the stores sold more expensive clothing for tourists. There were a couple art galleries that called themselves design studios with paintings, glass and pottery. We arrived at the famous nude statue at the harbor then turned north by the

City Hall to the Senate Square with the Senate building, a cathedral and the University of Helsinki. It was about three blocks back to the hotel.

It was Sunday morning and there were not very many people out. In Senate Square there was a Quecha group from Peru singing and selling CDs. Several busses of people from the local communities in native dress were arriving in town for a parade.

Swifts (Apus *apus*) were darting above the square and both Black-headed Gulls (Larus ridibundus) and Common Gulls (Larus canus) cruised the harbor and the Esplanade. I also saw a couple of Hooded Crows (Corvus corone), a few House Sparrows (Passer domesticus), a Tree Sparrow (Passer montanus) and a Magpie (Pica pica). I heard several Robins (Erithacus rubecula) in the trees in the arboretum.

The guide told us that Helsinki had about 500,000 people with another 500,000 in the GMA with about 6 million total for Finland. A condo downtown would run about 500,000€. Taxes ran about 80% but included medical coverage and education for everyone.

I stopped at a public toilet (WC) and paid a half Euro (about a buck) for its use. Clean. Three Western toilets and urinals.

Back from the walk Carol and I went out looking for a place for lunch. I suggested Finnish food but we stopped for Italian. I ordered a pepperoni pizza and a local beer. The beer was good but the pepperoni was more like sliced ham and there were big al dente slices of green pepper. Different.

Down near the harbor was a flea market with fresh fruits and vegetables from Spain, Germany, and Italy. There were a lot of other booths selling local crafts, furs, souvenirs, etc. Strawberries from the Ukraine were 5€ a kilo.

Back at the hotel we skipped supper. About 2200 I went down to the bar for a Coke light and a tonic. These were 4.5€ (6$) each.

21 Jun. Monday. I wanted to visit the Soumemlina Island fort or the zoo but Carol said it was too cold and rainy and wanted to see some museums. We checked and found most of the museums were closed on Monday. (I should have remembered that Monday is the universal down day for museums.) We tried to go to Tallinn the capitol of Estonia and a UNESCO Heritage site but the tour was cancelled. Tallinn was about 50 miles south across the Gulf of Finland.

We went shopping and had lunch in the Mount Everest, a Nepalese place. I had baby shrimp in capisum sauce. Good flavor but not very hot.

After lunch Carol had to get her hair done so I took off for the botanical garden.

I cut through a public park with statues, tennis courts, soccer fields, and play grounds to a gate leading into the garden. A couple Lilacs bushes had a Tree Sparrow hopping amongst the branches. Field Roses (<u>Rosa</u> <u>glabra</u>) were growing in the fence rows.

The botanical gardens belonged to Helsinki University. The grounds were open. Only the greenhouses have admission but they were closed on Monday. Trails led all directions and most of the specimen plants were labeled.

A large black <u>Aedes</u> mosquito landed on my hand. It was as large as our Gulf Coast salt marsh mosquito. Quiet and did not sting when it bit. There was also a yellow butterfly, <u>Gonepteryx</u> <u>rhamni</u>. A Lilac had a Tree Sparrow hopping amongst the branches. A large fat Wood Pigeon (<u>Columbua</u> <u>palumbus</u>) was feeding on the trail. Common weeds: Hawthorn (<u>Crategus</u> <u>monogyna</u>). Sheppard's purse (<u>Capsella</u> <u>bursa-pastoris</u>). Whitlow grass (<u>Draba</u> <u>muralis</u>). Plantain (<u>Plantago</u> <u>major</u>). Heath Bedstraw (<u>Gallium</u> <u>saxatile</u>). Giant Hogweed (<u>Heracleum</u> <u>mantegazzianum</u>). Chickweed (<u>Cerastium</u> sp.). Silverweed (<u>Potentilla</u> <u>anserina</u>). Sun Spurge (<u>Euphorbia</u> <u>helioscopia</u>). Red Clover (<u>Trifolium</u> <u>pretense</u>). Black Medic (<u>Medicago</u> <u>lupulina</u>). Meadow Vetchling (<u>Lathyrus</u> <u>pratensis</u>). Tufted Vetch (<u>Vicia</u> <u>cracca</u>). Cattail (<u>Typha</u> latifolia). Duckweed (<u>Lemna</u> <u>minor</u>). Yellow Water-lily (<u>Nuphur</u> <u>lutea</u>). Cotton Thistle (<u>Onopordum</u> <u>acanthium</u>). Wall Lettuce (<u>Mycelis</u> <u>muralis</u>). Dandelion (<u>Taraxacum</u> Sect <u>vulgaria</u>). Corn Marigold (<u>Chrysanthemum</u> <u>segetum</u>). Fewerfew (<u>Tanscetum</u> <u>parthenium</u>). Bulbous Buttercup (<u>Ranunculus</u> bulbosus). I did not get off the beaten path to feed the mosquitoes so these plants are from roadside, bottom of walls, cracks, fence lines, ditches, and other waste places.

22 Jun. Tuesday. This morning we had a tour to an old village called Porvoo and a Romanoff villa. The road was through Taiga mixed forest and wet meadows. Wild Lupine (<u>Lupinus</u> <u>nootkatensis</u>). Aspen (<u>Populus</u> <u>tremula</u>). Birch (<u>Betula</u> <u>pendula</u>). Alder shrubs (<u>Alnus</u> <u>glutinosa</u>). Various willows (<u>Salix</u> sp.). Lots of little yellow and white composites. Celery-leaved Buttercup (<u>Ranunculus</u> <u>sceleratus</u>), Alpine Pennycress (<u>Thiaspi</u> <u>alpestre</u>), Marsh Violet (Viola <u>palustris</u>), and white umbellifers lined the roads.

Houses were white and had steep roofs to control snow accumulation and many roofs had ladders to allow access for snow clearing. Barns were mostly painted red with steep metal roofs. All the fields had windbreaks of conifers. No crops had been planted yet.

Porvoo is the second oldest community in Finland. Located at the head of a quiet bay this old Hansiatic port town it is over 500 years old. It was about 50km of good road from Helsinki and served as a bedroom community. Population is about 48,000. Two of its most famous personalities were the painter Albert Edelfelt and the poet Johan Ludvig Runesberg.

Porvoo

Our tour of Old Town began when the bus let us off near the old historic Evangelistic Lutheran cathedral. The city and cathedral was burned several times. The last time the cathedral was burned was May of 2006. It was rebuilt and rededicated six months later. The church is located on the highest point in town.

Finland is officially bilingual but 94% speak Finnish and only 6%Swedish.

We left the church and walked down the cobblestone street between Technicolor to the square. One neat invention was the periscope on each house that allowed the householder to see who was coming along the street. The Empire style houses of Old Town were historic buildings under UNESCO protection. The street windows decorated shadow box style with personal items and lace curtains.

A pair of hooded crows was foraging in someone's back yard.

We left the square passing the remaining houses and the red boat houses along the river to the bus. Once we were all accounted for we drove through the more modern residential areas and past the industrial area where publishing, electronics and plastics were primary industries. Condos ran about 500,000€ (about a million bucks.)

We left for tea at Hikuld Manor a former Romanoff manor house that had been abandoned but recently converted to a teahouse and exclusive retreat. The walls were covered with pictures of the Romanoff family. <u>Valerianella</u> <u>locusta</u> grew in the lawn.

Back at the hotel we packed up to head for the airport. Since we would not leave for two hours I went looking for some allergy stuff for local fungus and pollen. I was directed to a pharmacy and the pharmacist who spoke English found a package of Zyrtec. I asked for some naprosin (Aleve) and was told this was a prescription drug because of liver damage.

We boarded an Air Russia 767 for St Petersburg about 200 miles east. There had been a catastrophic crash in the recent past and Russia had revoked the charter for 19 regional airlines. Only a few were still flying.

Ninety minutes later we were at St Petersburg Pulkovo airport. The airport was well mowed with no birds,

23 Jun. Wednesday. After immigration we were picked up and taken to the ship several miles from downtown. This was on the upstream side of the 700 city bridges and near the new high rise bridge that could handle ocean going ships. We found our assigned cabin, went to supper and crashed for the night.

In the morning there was a buffet breakfast followed by a trip briefing and a tour at 1100 to the Hermitage.

This former Romanoff palace is now an outstanding art and history museum with fabulous grounds with flowers and fountains. This was commissioned by Elizabeth I as her winter palace. It has been renovated numerous times but the throne room and the ballrooms have retained much of the character and opulence of the original design. There are five interconnected palaces: the Winter Palace, the Little Hermitage, the Old and New Hermitages often grouped as the Large Hermitage, and the Hermitage Theatre. It contains about three million exhibits in 328,000 sq. ft. Only about 5% of the items are on display.

We went directly to the Winter Palace 2nd floor second displays including works by da Vinci, Titian, Michelangelo, Rubens, Cezanne, van Gogh, and Picasso. Walls and ceilings and even the floors were works of art in themselves. There was a lot of gold leaf and gold-colored epoxy that replaced tarnished and missing gold leaf. I was a bit disappointed that we.

Hermitage

skipped the early Russian displays the Malachite Hall and the Florentine art. I guess we still saw a lot in the hour allowed by the old Russian ladies who controlled the traffic flow through the galleries.

Carol was concerned because there was no hand rail and the steps were uneven height. This occurred all during the trip. I guess 200 years ago the Romanoffs were spry and healthy and there were no handicapped laws.

Four starlings (<u>Sturnus</u> <u>vulgaris</u>) were hunting bugs in the grass near the landing. Plants included clovers, Blue-eyed Mary (<u>Omphalodes</u> <u>verna</u>), Horehound (<u>Marrubium</u> <u>vulgare</u>), vetch and dandelions.

On Wednesday afternoon we drove around downtown and through the Winter Palace museum. An evening entertainment a trip went to the Marlinsky Theatre for the St. Petersburg opera doing Swan Lake. No pictures allowed. We had folding chair wall seats sitting sideways similar to watching from an airplane window. The opera might have been a good dress rehearsal but was nothing I would shown the public.

Gas was 20 Rubles per liter or about $2.50/gallon. Waste Management International garbage trucks were doing their refuse thing. The streets were officially three lanes but there was often occupied by five lanes of traffic. Street sweepers were busy at night. Parking was prohibited but not enforced so there was often congestion. Lots of abandoned vehicles.

There were a lot of English speakers. Kids get two years of English beginning in grade six and are often anxious to practice.

Back by the ship were four Garganey ducks (<u>Anus</u> <u>querquedula</u>) with buff breast and white eye stripe checking out the waterline.

I hope no one hopes for a short history of Russia or details about the museums. This information is readily available in books and on the Internet. There is so much to see that it would take days to see any one of the museums. What I present is cultural observations and best guess on plant and bird identifications.

24 Jun. Thursday. Our objective for the day was Peterhof or Petrodvorets about 20 mile west on the Gulf of Finland. This was the site of the "cabin" built by Peter the Great to oversee the construction of Kronshtadt naval base Russia's door to Europe. He liked it so much commissioned Monplaisir, a baroque style summer palace in 1714. He wanted something that would be better than Versailles. Over the years he built several palaces with the whole estate being called Peterhof. The buildings and grounds are outstanding particularly the fountain facing the sea. The art and the gold leaf everything was impressive. Again we only went to the Grand Palace and upper garden in our hour. The old Russian ladies are efficient at keeping the traffic moving. Visitor lines extended around the block as we left.

It was overcast with an intermittent slow fine rain. The rain was cool indicating spring had sprung and the cold winter rain was over. In another few weeks the summer would begin with temperatures in the 80s.

On the way back to the bus we stopped for a Coke Lite and a beer. The beer cost less than the Coke and disappointed me. It had a Russian label and a Budweiser cap. 8000 miles to drink a Bud.

Peterhof

I noticed a difference in the vehicle traffic between Helsinki and Russia. Helsinki had many newer Western cars and trucks. Russia had a lot of older Russian models cars and a lot more trucks.

Next tour was the Catherine Palace in Pushkin. It was all so fast. My favorite was the rebuilt amber room. No pictures allowed.

We stopped at an upscale gift shop. Lots of contemporary and modern art. The gift shop had good quality art for sale. I asked about some amber with insects and was told it had been molded. I took out my UV light and showed the clerk the lines showing the layers.

There were also some good modern art and scenes of Russia. Prices ran from several hundred to $7,000 US. I asked how the prices were fixed and was told it was based on size and reputation of the artist. They had never heard of the square inch method.

Matryoshka dolls ran from about $20 to $200 depending on number of dolls and subject. They did not originate in Russia but became famous in Russia. These are nested wooden dolls made from seasoned pine and hand painted in various subjects. We have one showing Russian leaders and another showing Bart Simpson figures but most were Russian women and children. Papier-mâché figures and containers were also popular.

On the way back to the ship there were ditches with cattails (Typha sp) and puddles of standing water with duckweed (Lemna sp). Two Thistle species were along the road. These looked like multi-headed Creeping Thistle (Cirsium arvense) and large single headed Woolly Thistle (C. eriophorum).

There were several small alters with flowers along the road probably commemorating traffic deaths.

A common sidewalk flower was Gold of Pleasure (Camelina sativa). Lots of clover. Patches of Fire Weed (Epilobium angustifolium) locally called Rosebay Willowherb. Common Sorrel (Rumex acetosa) grew in fence lines. There was an isolated patch of Black Medic (Medicago lupulina).

25 Jun. Friday. This afternoon a canal cruise was scheduled. There are scheduled water taxis but these private vessels built for tours. The boats were about 15X60 feet and the front half was covered by a transparent cover. Some of the many creeks and small rivers had been filled in or diverted through pipes or dug out to form major transportation canals crossed by numerous bridges. The tour entered the Fontanka R. and followed along two canals to the Moika R. and rejoined the Fontanka crossing under about fifteen bridges. There were no house boats but there were plenty of work boats and water taxis. We passed under the "laundry bridge" and past the Peter's summer palace and the summer park.

The guide said about 70% of downtown was under UNESCO protection so no highrise buildings.

Verain (Verbena officinalis) and Cut-leaf Self-heal (Prunella laciniata) and White Horehound (Marrubium vulgare) were near the canal cruise landing.

A Collared Turtle Dove (Streptopelia decoato) flew across the river. It crashed through the air like our Whitewing Doves.

On the way back to the ship a big stretch limo with flowers on the hood was parked along the river. The bride and groom pictures were being photographed along the river. In Russian weddings there was just one official bridesmaid and best man but a lot of guests. Females out number males about 60/40 so the brides were lucky. We still saw several wedding parties that afternoon.

We passed a Ford dealership and a motorcycle shop that displayed several brands. There were used cars on sale for 130,000 Rubles (about $4,000). I don't know what the average income is. There were not very many scooters or motorcycles on the streets. Too cold? Too expensive?

We stopped on the north side of the river at the Spit of Vasilyevsky for a good view of down town. There were two large maritime monuments. Then we drove past the Russian Navy training cruiser Aurora. This ship had fired the first shot against the Czar in 1917.

Several men were fishing from the banks. Since there were about 30 species in the river I wonder what they were catching. The river bank has been stabilized with granite blocks. Maximum depth is about 100 feet. The river is frozen over from September to March.

Not enough time to see so much. No time for the zoo, botanical garden, many specialized museums such as the vodka museum. It might have been more fruitful to have had a hotel in down town.

Back aboard ship there was tea time and at 1900 we left up the Neva River for the next stop, Mandrogi. There was a bon voyage cocktail party with the crew and a briefing on what to see at Mandrogi. Dinner was at 2000.

26 Jun. Saturday. Verchnie Mandrogi was a thriving village with mining forestry and cottage industries before Peter the Great. During WWII the village was destroyed. It has been rebuilt as a sort of Disney collective beginning in 1996. It has a summer education facility for children. Its tourist facilities attracted local visitors and its tourist attractions are a stopover for cruise ships on the Volga/Baltic waterway. They sell handmade crafts and food. Tour time was scheduled for 1.5 hours.

On Saturday morning there was an exercise program in yoga-like Qi-Dong followed by a Russian class and a cooking demonstration and a lecture on what to look for in Russian souvenirs.

Mandrogi

Breakfast began at 0700. A few people were dressed casually but most were jeans. Most of the women did not carry a purse although some had fanny packs.

We were crossing Lake Ladoga the largest freshwater lake in Europe. It was gouged by glaciers during the last Ice Age to a depth of 754 feet. It covers almost 7,000 square miles. Tankers and barge traffic plied the lake. The lake was large enough that we were out of sight of land.

About 0900 in the southeast corner of the lake we passed through the first lock and entered the Svir River. There were two locks dropping 27 m (about 90 ft) to enter Lake Onega. The river reminded me of the Inland Passage with the trees flying past. The ship was cruising about 12 knots.

A Magpie (<u>Pica</u> <u>pica</u>) flew over as we waited for the lock. There was Coot (<u>Fulica</u> <u>atra</u>) and a small flock of small black ducks.

Vegetation included Silver and Downy Birch (<u>Betula</u> <u>pendula</u> and <u>pubescens</u>), Aspen (<u>Aspen</u> <u>tremula</u>), Grey Popular (<u>Populus</u> <u>canescens</u>), Bay and Osier Willows (<u>Salix</u> <u>pentandra</u> and <u>viminalis</u>).

There were scattered gulls mostly Common Gulls and what looked and acted like a Kingfisher (<u>Alcedo</u> <u>atthis</u>).

Along the river the sun broke out and the air temperature as about 60°. Several fishermen were out in raft-like boats along the channel edge.

Dachas

Dachas appeared along the shore. This was land given to the people for garden plots. Most are now occupied by houses and maybe a garden. Some of the houses are shacks and some are mansions but most are middleclass. Many built on the water have boat houses or saunas or both.

The Mandrogi tour was from 1515 to 1645. It was overcast with impending rain. We checked the local shopping and found several items unique to Mandrogi. Weaving and embroidery. Handmade jewelry. Wood carving. Matryoshkas. We tried some of the berry pies.

There were a number of Bank Swallows cleaning up on the afternoon mosquitoes and midges.

There were a lot wetland plants. Grass of Parnassus (Parnassia palustris). Sheppard's Purse. Common Whitlow Grass (Erpphila verna). Lesser Swinecress (Coronopus didymus). Black Mustard (Brassica nigra). Chickweed (Stellaria media). Mouse ears (Cerastium arvense). Common Sorrel (Rumex acetosa). Heath Bedstraw (Gallium saxatile). Sawwort (Serratula tinctoria). Plantago (Plantago major). Yellow Oxalis (Oxalis corniculata). Red Clover. White Clover. Yellow Oxalis (Oxalis corniculata). Fireweed (Epilobium angustifolium). Tufted Vetch (Vicia cracca). Wild Lupine (Lupinus nootkatensis).

Small boats were drifting and fishing. Even a cabin cruiser was fishing.

Lake Onega is the second largest lake in Europe covering almost 4,000 square miles. It has a maximum depth of 380 feet and has about 1650 islands sprinkled across the lake. Fifty rivers enter the lake. The water is brownish from diatoms and other organics. There are about 40 species of fish. The north end of the lake is connected to the Beloye More or White Sea that connects to the Barents Sea and Arctic Ocean.

We turned north to Kihzi. After sailing all night through the twilight and a three-quarter moon we arrived at Kihzi about 0800.

27 Jun. Sunday. We turned north to Kihzi. After sailing all night through the twilight and a three-quarter moon we arrived at Kihzi about 0800. I was up and shot some pictures at 2AM. The moon. Vapors rising from the water.

White Night Twilight

It was mid June
Labrador was still freezing
And covered in snow
T'was twilight about 11PM
When the big red sun ball
Was sucked down into the black boreal trees
But the White Night twilight
Continued for another two hours
Until the sun climbed
Over the NE trees
Staining the clouds and the White Night
Orange-pink

*****

Six km long Kihzi Island was a pagan ritual site. It was settled eight hundred years ago by Russian colonists. It is now a living museum of colonial Russian structures including the Church of the Intercession and the Church of the Transfiguration with five concentric rings of domes. There were also farmhouses, barns, a mill and a bell tower moved from other islands or hand built of native lumber in the native way.

There was some grumbling about the weather. It was in the upper 50's with a tepid mist. What could be better than a misty subarctic spring morning with early spring flowers? At least there was a wooden boardwalk to keep your feet dry.

The farmhouse we visited reminded me much of the houses on the coast of Newfoundland. It was of single wall construction of native wood. Similar problems have similar solutions.

One major difference was the large stone stove between the kitchen and family areas used for heating, cooking and sleeping on top of. This must have come from Tartar roots similar to the Tibetan/Mongol kung. This house also had a sauna which the Newfoundland houses lacked.

Kihiz Farmhouse

Kihzi plants included most of those already listed plus Yellow Iris (Iris pseudacorus), Water Plantain (Alisma plantago-aquatica), Bluejoint Grass (Calamagrostis sp.) and Horse tails.

There were supposed to be vipers on the Island. I can see garter snakes but what kind of viper would be this far north on an island? Maaybe all snakes are called vipers.

We also looked at several churches and a windmill.

28 Jun. Monday. At the southern end of the lake we transited the 43 foot lock up into the Vytegra Canal with thick brown water due to runoff from logging operations. There are eight locks and hydroelectric generating plant then into the Kovaha River to White Lake (Lake Beloye). There were numerous small villages along all of the rivers with a few dachas and several small industrial sites.

Black-headed Gulls were around the locks but the Common Gull was common on the rivers. An Osprey (<u>Pandion</u> <u>haliaetus</u>) was sitting on a branch over the water. A Great Tit (<u>Parus</u> <u>major</u>) was flitting around in the trees. I could hear Robins (<u>Erithacus</u> <u>rubecula</u>) but could not see them. Out in the lake I saw a couple gulls mobbing something. This large white hawk was a Buzzard (<u>Buteo</u> <u>buteo</u>) sitting on a dead tree on a small islet.

Lake Beloye may have resulted from a meteor impact. It is clearly a circle and could well be an impact crater but many arctic lakes are circular. The area was first settled in the 8th century. In the 17th century it was designated as the Czars fishing grounds.

Our next stop was at Goritzy to visit the Krillo-Belozersky Monastery. The monastery was built by the Romanoffs for 200 monks and 200 trainees. We toured the monastery and the two cathedrals and heard some sacred music by a group of laymen.

The lake has a myth of increasing longevity of any one swimming in the cold waters. The water is sterile thanks to the presence of silver. I guess those kids swimming in the lake will live forever.

Birch, aspen, popular, Mountain Ash, lilac bushes, plantain, Common Mallow (Malva sylvestris) grew on the grounds.

There was a flock of Rooks (Corvus frugilegus) flying between the monastery and a copse of trees outside the walls. A few Hooded Crows were flying around the towers. A pair of Barred Warblers (Sylvia nisoria) was feeding along the road inside the gates.

We weighed anchor about 1600. There was vodka tasting party about 2300. Six different brands. They were all good except one with pepper and spices. I sat with a Canadian from Toronto and two Australians. They had a poor opinion of Bush but a good impression of Obama so far.

29 Jun. Tuesday. We left White Lake early in the evening through the Sheksna River locks as part of the Mariinsk Canal System. One item of interest was the remains of the 15th century church at Krokhino the creation of a hydroelectric plant lake.

The Mariinsk System was supposed to connect the Baltic to Caspian Sea transportation problem. Past Goritzy the Rybinsk Reservoir had been built to keep the rivers flowing. In the summer several large rivers including the Volga formerly dried up. In1932 Stalin implemented the "Great Volga Plan" where the Volga and the Sheksna Rivers were dammed and the big reservoir was formed flooding 700 villages.

We went up through two locks to enter the reservoir and down one lock into the Volga. This last lock at Rybinsk has the statue of Mother Volga. About 1500 we reached Yaroslavl.

I was up about 0400 and watched the fog coming off the river. The black trees silhouetted against the white night faded in and out as the fog surged and fell. Little islands with bushes flew by like ghosts. River temperature was 50°F with the air temperature of 55°F.

Russian Orthodox Church

Yaroslavl is a middle size city (population of 600,000) and a major port on the Volga. It was founded in the 11th century and survived numerous battles. Several major cathedrals were build in the 17th century and have been restored in the past couple decades.

We visited two cathedrals and went to an overlook where couples attached padlocks to the railing and tossed the keys in the river as a vow of eternal love. Back at the square we were let loose in a covered market with lots of good looking fresh fruits and vegetables and an adjacent open flea market with a lot of cheap clothing.

While heading for the main exit a frowsy gypsy about 30 with uncombed brown hair and a little girl stuck out her hand and asked for money. I told her "No" and was walking past when she gave me the bad eye and spat out a gypsy curse. Guess she took her begging seriously.

We stopped at several shops on the way back to the ship. The ship weighed anchor at 1900.

Yaroslavl

30 Jun. Wednesday. We sailed down the Volga all night and arrived at Uglich. Colorful domes were visible as we approached. Uglich does not have a Kremlin or fort wall. The village was founded in 1148. One claim to fame is the revolution was started here by Boris Godunov.

New vegetation was Good King Henry (<u>Chenopodium</u> <u>bonus-henricus</u>), Ragged Robin (<u>Lychnis</u> <u>flos-cuculi</u>), Common Sorrel (<u>Rumex</u> <u>acetosa</u>), and several small composites. Silverweed (<u>Potentilla</u> <u>anserine</u>), Black Mustard, Hogweed (<u>Heracleum</u> <u>sphondylium</u>), were growing in a swale. We visited a memorial park and a cathedral and more shopping. There was a factory outlet for watches made in the area. Carol bought two. I saw a replica of a WWII Russian Army pocket watch and fob for about $50 but I problem would not use it. We got a couple T-shirts and a Bart Simpson Matrioshka.

The evening was time for the Captains dinner. We sat with a couple from Phoenix. He thought the Arizona immigration was not tough enough. Global warming would not bother Phoenix because they were already hot.

1 Jul. Thursday. About sun up we entered the Moscow Canal about fours from Moscow. Weather was clear and near 70°. Radio reports said it had been 80° and people were dying of heat stroke and alcohol related drowning.

An Eared Grebe (<u>Podiceps</u> <u>nigricollis</u>) cruised along the channel edge.

As we approached Moscow there were more communities and some high rise buildings probably condos. The shore from the water's edge to the trees was short grass. There were benches and small docks and washed out areas where people picnicked, fished, sun bathed and swam. There were a lot of people on the river banks even on a week day.

Yellow water-Lilies (<u>Nuphar</u> <u>lutea</u>) with big heart-shaped leaves grew along the river edges. There were large patches of vetch about half way up the banks.

The morning activities consisted of a disembarkation briefing and the presentation to the tour video. They even managed to catch me a couple times.

Across the river were several expensive yachts and a private military museum which we could no visit. I saw a large ground Zubr Russian military hovercraft similar to our Marine assault boats.

A-90 Orlyonok or KM Ekranoplan Flarecraft

There was also a giant A-90 Orlyonok or KM Ekranoplan. This is a wing-in-ground effect (WIG) or flarecraft or seaskimmer and looks like a plane with short wings. This one was built in 1965 with ten turbojet engines. It was 347 feet long and 141 foot wing span and crashed in 1980. It was called the /Caspian Sea Monster.

Two ocean going racers in the million dollar range were playing on the river. Somebody has money!

We tied up about noon. A city tour was arranged for 1330 - a bus and walking tour around town and then to a concert and folk music demonstration of traditional instruments.

The tour showed Moscow to be a growing city with a mix of old and modern facilities. We walked through Red Square and drove past the Kremlin then through Moscow University. Moscow certainly does not look like I had expected from the spy novels and movies. I asked about James Bond tour but no such luck – you know:. US embassy, Gorky Park, KGB headquarters in Dzerzhinsky Square, Butyrskaya Prison.

We were dropped near Red Square (Red means beautiful and not the color or the bloodshed) and herded in through a gate attached to the national library. The former market square is maybe ten acres. St Basils

Cathedral was on the opposite end (built by Ivan the Terrible on his conversion).

White Night in Red Square

The big State Department Store GUM was to the left and the Kremlin wall and Lenin's tomb were on the right. Really not what I had expected. That Gum department was three floors of Dior and other high end stores (it used to be restricted to foreigners and government officials). Moscow was more modern than many European cities in not having the sky hidden by electrical wires.

GUM at night

After our box lunches we went to a musical presentation. Young musicians played the traditional Russian instruments very well.

2 Jul. Friday. This morning a trip to the Military Museum was scheduled. Outside was a heroic statue commemorating the Kursk submarine disaster. There were dioramas and displays of Russian military history from Stalingrad to the present. The displays had pictures and artifacts and original art works. One exhibit is wreckage and pictures of the U-2 that was shot down in 1960. At the end of the tour we had a demonstration of Russian weapons and got to handle them. Both the AK-47 and AK-74 are heavy at about 16 pounds loaded. On the outside was a display of rockets, guns, and military aircraft.

We made reservations for a "Moscow by Night" tour which I thought might include some of the famous Moscow entertainment. I was mistaken. It was roughly the same bus tour of town only in the dark. The only high spot was Red Square at night with the lighted department store and St Basils and lighted red stars on some of the buildings. I think a lot of people were disappointed.

3 Jul. Saturday. Early in the morning there was a thick cloud of smog to the northwest. Peat and forest fires were burning. Drought killed most of the wheat crop and the fields were being burned. (A week after we returned on July 4th smog blanketed Moscow and the temperature hit 98°F the highest since 1938 and Stalin was in power. By 1 Aug the temp hit 104°F the highest since temperatures were recorded – 150 years.)

Saturday was the last full day of the cruise. We had the opportunity to go into town for a couple hours. Since neither of us read nor speak Russian we decided to pass on that. Although many Russians speak English I would imagine there would be a lot of dissatisfaction with the best job using their language skill was selling souvenirs and sodas on the street.

We went to the Kremlin and the Armory. Kremlin means fort. The Moscow Kremlin is located on one of Moscow's seven hills. It started as a fortified village and by the 14th century it was filled with churches, monasteries, and manor houses. Currently it contains 17 cathedrals and all of the major legislative and executive quarters and offices although none of the quarters are in use. One of the features is the world's largest canon (It was never fired). The world's largest bell also sits in the Kremlin (It was never rung). We passed the KGB headquarters but it is outside the Kremlin. From the descriptions of writers like le Carre and Fleming I would guess they were never in Moscow.

Outside the Kremlin was a grassy park filled with picnickers. Vegetation included Daisy (<u>Bellis</u> <u>perennis</u>), Linden trees, and Mountain Ash.

In general the people look happy and surviving. I did not see any suits but then there were no ragged troops except teenagers that looked like teens anywhere. Lots of pretty girls.

The military looks young. There was compulsory service for 2 years, then 18 months, and now a year. The head of the Army said Russia does not have a professional Army with only 27% career officers and 34% career enlisted.

Other than the one farmers market I did not see prices on ordinary food and clothes. We discussed the price for homes but this did not account for the majority of Russians.

Apparently many people want democracy but not jammed down their throats. They want freedom but don't want to pay the price of abandoning communism and socialism. Some still think Stalin was a good guy.

Kremlin

After we returned we had our bill for the cruise and paid up. There was a farewell dinner of Russian style food. Boiled potatoes with sauce. *Borsch* (beet soup). *Pelmeni* (dumplings but without vinegar). *Chay* (tea but not served with jelly). *Pelmeni* was available from street vendors but our guides recommended against eating street food.

4 Jul. Sunday. We packed up ready to go and set the bags out in the passageway. Our bus out to the airport was scheduled to leave at 0800. It was a two hour drive to Domodedovo airport. We stood in line a half hour waiting for our boarding passes then went through a whole-body scanner and on to the boarding gate. The scanner was neat. No undressing. Just stand still in this big glass tube. We did remove our shoes and put on disposable slippers while the shoes were x-rayed.

The 767-300 left on time. We jumped into broken clouds and flew NW across Lake Ladoga and southern Finland and were above the clouds to New York. Customs and immigration were at Dulles. There was a four hour layover before our flight to San Antonio. We were in the house by 2100.

Retrospect

In general the trip was interesting. I learned a lot. Geography. Botany. Birds. History. I would recommend some changes in the tour.

The ship could be improved by: a. fixing the air conditioning; b. changing from duvets to sheets and blankets; c. taking the sharp edges off the metal molding on the stairs; d. changing emphasis on food from looks to taste since most of the customers were from the US or Canada.

I recommend more choice in tours since there are numerous museums, parks, battle grounds in instead of one size fits all. I also recommend including some local food on some of the tours and having someone familiar with the local ecology.

Legend
H = Helsinki, S = St Petersburg, M = Moscow

Biologicals

Birds

Podicipedidae
Eared Grebe (<u>Podiceps</u> <u>nigricollis</u>)   Moscow Canal
Lariformes
Black-headed Gulls (<u>Larus</u> <u>ridibundus</u>)   H, locks
Common Gulls (<u>Larus</u> <u>canus</u>)   H, Neva, rivers
Anatidae
Garganey ducks (<u>Anus</u> <u>querquedula</u>)   S
Accipitridae
Buzzard (<u>Buteo</u> <u>buteo</u>)   Vytegra Canal
Pandionidae
Osprey (<u>Pandion</u> <u>haliaetus</u>)   Kihzi, Lake Beloye
Rallidae
Coot (<u>Fulica</u> <u>atra</u>)   Svir R.
Columbidae
Wood Pigeon (<u>Columbua</u> <u>palumbus</u>)   H
Collared Turtle Dove (<u>Streptopelia</u> <u>decoato</u>)   S
Apodiformes
Swifts (<u>Apus</u> *apus*)   H
Alcedinidae
Kingfisher (<u>Alceo</u> <u>atthis</u>)   Lake Ladogad
Hirundinidae
Bank Swallow (<u>Riparia</u> <u>riparia</u>)   rivers
Sylviidae
Barred Warbler <u>Sylvia</u> <u>nisoria</u>
Turdidae
Robins (<u>Erithacus</u> <u>rubecula</u>)   H, Kihzi, Lake Beloye
Paridae
Great Tit (<u>Parus</u> <u>major</u>)   Kihzi, Lake Beloye
Ploceidae
House Sparrows (<u>Passer</u> <u>domesticus</u>)   H

Tree Sparrow (Passer montanus)   H
Sturnidae
Starlings (Sturnus vulgaris)   S
Corvidae
Hooded Crows (Corvus corone)   H, various
Magpie (Pica pica)   H, Svir R.

Insects
Clouded Sulfur Gonepteryx rhamni   H
Aedes sp.   Various
Aglais urticae   Uglich

Plants

Ferns
Rock Polypody (<u>Polypodium</u> <u>virginianum</u>)   Kihzi.
Equisetaceae
Common Horsetail (<u>Equisetum</u> <u>arvense</u>)   Kihzi.
Meadow Horsetail (<u>Equisetum</u> <u>pretense</u>)   Kihzi.
Pinaceae
European Larch (<u>Larix</u> <u>decidua</u>)   various
Ulmaceae
Wych Elm (<u>Ulmus</u> <u>glabra</u>)   H
Salicaceae
Bay Willows (<u>Salix</u> <u>pentandra</u>)   various
Osier Willow (<u>Salix</u> <u>viminalis</u>)   various
Various willows (Salix sp.)   various
Aspen (<u>Populus</u> <u>tremula</u>)   various
Grey Popular (<u>Populus</u> <u>canescens</u>)   various
Betulaceae
Silver Birch (<u>Betula</u> <u>pendula</u>)   various
Alder shrubs (<u>Alnus</u> <u>glutinosa</u>)   various
Downy Birch (<u>Betula</u> <u>pubescens</u>)   S
Platanaceae
London Plane trees (<u>Platanus</u> <u>hybrida</u>)   H
Hippocastanaceae
Horse Chestnut (<u>Aesculus</u> <u>hippocastanum</u>)   H
Tillaceae
Linden (<u>Tilia</u> <u>cordata</u>)   H
Polygonaceae
Common Sorrel (<u>Rumex</u> <u>acetosa</u>)   S
Chenopodiaceae
Good King Henry (<u>Chenopodium</u> <u>bonus-henricus</u>)   Yaroslavl
Caryophyllaceae
Chickweed (<u>Stellaria</u> sp.)   various
Arctic Mouse ears (<u>Cerastium</u> <u>arctiana</u>)   various
Ragged Robin (<u>Lychnis</u> <u>flos-cuculi</u>)   Yaroslavl
Nymphaceae
Yellow Water-lily (<u>Nuphur</u> <u>lutea</u>)   S, M

Ranunculaceae

Bulbous Buttercup (<u>Ranunculus</u> <u>bulbosus</u>)	H
Celery-leaved Buttercup (<u>Ranunculus</u> <u>sceleratus</u>)	

Cruciferae

Alpine Pennycress (<u>Thiaspi</u> <u>alpestre</u>)	Porvoo
Sheppard's purse (<u>Capsella</u> <u>bursa-pastoris</u>)	various
Whitlow grass (<u>Draba</u> <u>muralis</u>)	various
Common Whitlow Grass (<u>Erophila</u> <u>verna</u>)	various
Lesser Swinecress (<u>Coronopus</u> <u>didymus</u>)	various
Black Mustard (<u>Brassica</u> <u>nigra</u>)	various
Gold of Pleasure (<u>Camelina</u> <u>sativa</u>)	S

Parnassiaceae

Grass of Parnassus (<u>Parnassia</u> <u>palustris</u>)	Kihzi

Rosaceae

Field Rose (<u>Rosa</u> <u>arvensis</u>)	H
Hawthorn (<u>Crategus</u> <u>monogyna</u>)	H
Dog Rose (<u>Rosa</u> <u>canina</u>)	H, Kihzi.
Silverweed (<u>Potentilla</u> <u>anserina</u>)	various
Mountain Ash or Rowan (<u>Sorbus</u> <u>aucuparia</u>)	H, M

Leguminosae

Red Clover (<u>Trifolium</u> <u>pretense</u>)	various
White Clover (<u>Trifolium</u> <u>repens</u>)	various
Black Medic (<u>Medicago</u> <u>lupulina</u>)	various
Meadow Vetchling (<u>Lathyrus</u> <u>pratensis</u>)	H
Tufted Vetch (<u>Vicia</u> <u>cracca</u>)	various
Wild Lupine (<u>Lupinus</u> <u>nootkatensis</u>)	various

Oxalidaceae

Yellow Oxalis (<u>Oxalis</u> <u>corniculata</u>)	various

Linaceae

Perennial Flax (<u>Linum</u> <u>perenne</u>)	

Geraniaceae

Meadow Cranesbill (<u>Geranium</u> <u>pretense</u>)	Kihzi.

Euphorbiaceae

Sun Spurge (<u>Euphorbia</u> <u>helioscopia</u>)	H, Kihzi.

Violaceae

Marsh Violet (<u>Viola</u> <u>palustris</u>)	Porvoo

Onagraceae
Rosebay Willowherb or Fireweed (<u>Epilobium</u>
<u>angustifolium</u>) various

Umbelliferae

Giant Hogweed (<u>Heracleum</u> <u>mantegazzianum</u>)	various
Fennel (<u>Foeniculun</u> <u>vulgare</u>)	various
Stone Parsley (<u>Sison</u> <u>amomom</u>)	various

Rubiaceae

Heath Bedstraw (<u>Gallium</u> <u>saxatile</u>)	various
Common Cleavers (<u>Gallium</u> <u>aparine</u>)	various

Boraginaceae

Blue-eyed Mary (<u>Omphalodes</u> <u>verna</u>)	S

Verbenaceae

Verain (<u>Verbena</u> <u>officinalis</u>)	S

Labiatae

Cut-leaf Self-heal (<u>Prunella</u> <u>laciniata</u>)	S
Catmint (<u>Nepata</u> <u>cateria</u>)	S
Nettle (<u>Urtica</u> <u>dioica</u>)	Kihzi.

Plantaginaceae

Plantain (<u>Plantago</u> <u>major</u>) various	
Water Plantain (Alisma plantago-aquatica)	Kizhi

Valerianaceae

<u>Valerianella locusta</u>	Porvoo

Campanulaceae

Spreading Bellflower (<u>Campanula</u> <u>patula</u>)	H

Compositae

Daisy (<u>Bellis perennis</u>)	Moscow
Scentless Mayweed (<u>Matricaria</u> <u>perforate</u>)	
Ox-eye Daisy (<u>Leucanthemum</u> <u>vulgare</u>)	
Cotton Thistle (<u>Onopordum</u> <u>acanthium</u>)	S
Dandelion (<u>Taraxacum</u> Sect <u>vulgaria</u>)	various
Corn Marigold (<u>Chrysanthemum</u> <u>segetum</u>)	S
Fewerfew (<u>Tanscetum</u> <u>parthenium</u>)	various
Creeping Thistle (<u>Cirsium</u> <u>arvense</u>)	S
Woolly Thistle (<u>C</u>. <u>eriophorum</u>)	S
Sawwort (<u>Serratula</u> <u>tinctoria</u>)	Kihzi
Wall Lettuce (<u>Mycelis</u> <u>muralis</u>)	various

Iridaceae
Yellow Iris (<u>Iris</u> <u>pseudacorus</u>)   Kihzi
Lemnaceae
Duckweed (<u>Lemna</u> <u>minor</u>)   H, S
Typhaceae
Cattail (<u>Typha</u> <u>latifolia</u>)   various
Graminae
Northern Reed Grass (<u>Calamagrostis</u> <u>inexposa</u>)   Kizhi
Bluejoint Grass (<u>Calamagrostis</u> sp.)   Kizhi

White Night, Taiga and Foggy River

Hope you enjoyed a taste of Russia. *Da svi danya.*

Vietnam and Cambodia

Carl Lahser

24 Oct to 10 Nov 2011

Vietnam and Cambodia

The Dream.

In Sep 2010, my wife, Carol, and I discussed taking a trip in late 2011. Maybe Africa? Maybe Australia and/or New Zealand? We looked at the programs of several tour companies and finally settled on a 16 day tour on AMA Waterways with a flight to Hanoi, a junk cruise on Ha Long Bay, a flight to Siem Reap, visits to Angkor archeological sites, then by ship across Tonle Sap Lake and down the Tonle Sap River to Kampong Chhang wetlands, Kampong Tralach, Oudong, Phnom Penh, and into the Mekong River Delta to Ho Chi Minh City. We picked October 2011, as it is the end of the wet season and not quite so hot.

*****

Itemized upfront cost:

Land tour	$4,198 ea
Travel insurance	$ 295 ea
Continental to Houston and Tokyo	
Japan Airline to Hanoi	
return from Ho Chi Minh City	$1,678 ea
Transfers and local air fare	$1,398 ea
Total	$7,569 ea

Then there will be tips, taxes, and purchases

*****

Background.

Back in ancient times (1940's), I learned of Indo China from reading Terry and the Pirates in the Sunday comics. Somewhere in the back of my mind has lived a desire to see Rangoon, Hanoi, Saigon, and the Angkor temples. I was in the Air Force Reserves and did not get sent to Vietnam during the "police action". Since then I have been to Hong Kong, China, Macao, Japan, Taiwan, Korea, and Guam but not to the Philippines or Vietnam.

Homework.

Reference books include:

The Vietnam Guidebook. Barbara Cohen (1971).
Treasures and Pleasures of Vietnam and Cambodia. Impact Guide (2002)
Vietnam, Laos, & Cambodia Handbook. Passport Books (1996)
Guide to Angkor, Asia Books, Dawn Rooney (1994).
Angkor – Splendors of the Khmer Civilization, Asia Books Marilla Albanese (2006)
Plant Life of the Pacific World. The Infantry Journal. Elmer D. Merrill (1945)
Handy Pocket Guide to Tropical Plants by E. Chan
A Field Guide to Tropical Plants of Asia by David Engel
Tropical Plants of Asia. Timber. David Engel and S. Phummai (2000)
Birds of Southeast Asia. Princeton. Morten Strange (2000).
Hong Kong Birds by Viney and Phillipps.
Golden Bones by Sichan Siv

There were also a number of Internet sites on plants, seashells, and butterflies of China, Manchuria, Korea, Vietnam, Singapore, Malaysia, and the Philippines. Several titles are out of print or cost $100 or more.

*****

Getting Ready.

We began preparations a year early. Tour tickets and plane reservations. Passports. Check inoculations and get whatever is required. Apply for visas 90 days before we leave. Trip insurance. The tour company has the tour well planned.

For me the planning and preparation for a trip is fun and a learning experience in itself. It should be an important part of any trip. Of course, like an old English traveler said, if you do your research well there is really no reason to visit exotic places. This is probably true but I'll go if I get the opportunity.

My procedure for any trip is as follows: make a chronological picture record and chronological tape recordings to create a trip report; add lists of birds and plants seen and identified - many would be identified on site while others would be identified later from pictures. Most of the plants I will see are assumed to be ornamentals, agricultural crops, and invasives with only a few natives. Birds will be recorded where seen. Hopefully, there will be some trips out of towns.

I checked with the Air Force Office of Special Investigations (AFOSI). I got their latest anti-terrorism briefing and found the terrorist threat for Vietnam and Cambodia to be moderate. Several travel security sites recommended only standard situational awareness with no special precautions.

I checked the medical area intelligence reports for Vietnam, Laos and Cambodia in the Monthly Disease Occurrence (World- wide), reviewed the Disease Vector Ecology Profiles (DVEP) prepared by the Defense Pest Management Information Center, and called the Communicable Disease Center (CDC) [(800) 232-4636] and CDC Malaria Hotline [(707) 488-7100]. They listed TB, dengue, malaria, and chloera as endemic and measles, chickenpox, hepatitis A and B, polio, HIV/AIDS, and bird flu plus a few others in rural or agricultural or other unique situations. Basic sanitation and mosquito and fly control have greatly reduced diseases in the cities.

In late August a typhoon rolled over Vietnam and Cambodia. Saigon and Hanoai were hit with 80 km winds, Laos was flooded and 200 tourists were evacuated from the Angor area. There were about 3000 deaths along the Mekong. Two weeks later Typhoon Nesat ran over the Phillipines and Hainan Island then into southern China. Two weeks later, 3 Oct, Typhoon Nalgae hit a little further north in China and sucked the monsoon northeast into Thailand and Laos causing widespread flooding.

Ten days before we were to leave the tour company notified us that we would take a bus from Siem Reap around Tongle Sap Lake and board the ship at Kampong Cham. The lake and the Mekong were up about 20 feet. I was hoping to see the floating rice and marsh birds along the lake.

Cambodia 's recovery from the US bombing during the Vietnam War, the Khmer Rouge, civil war and a long history of poverty and corruption has been largely due to clothing manufacturing. There are 300 registered garment factories with 70% of exports coming to the US. At the beginning of 2011 Cambodia increased the minimum wage to $61 per month but still less than the $93 average living cost. Twenty percent of the wages go to support the family farm. Many of the workers put in overtime to earn an extra $50 a month to cover $15-25 for rent, $5-10 for utilities plus food, drinking water and transportation. Food costs average $1.25 a day but workers often have only $4 a month available.

Working conditions are poor inspite of what we saw with about 3,000 workers reported to have lost consciousness in 17 separate mass-fainting incidents at 12 garment factories. Poor ventilation. Hazardous chemicals. Long hours. Malnutrition. Corrupt unions fighting amongst themselves. Large international companies taking advantage and pressuring the workers, businesses, and the government. All this not readily visible to the casual visitor.

*****

Physical Setting.

Vietnam is a long narrow S-shaped country lying between the Tropic of Cancer and the equator. China and the Gulf of Tonkin is to the north, the Pacific Ocean to the east, and the Gulf of Thailand is on the south. It is less than half the size of California. Cambodia (Kampuchea) and Laos border it on the west.

The Truong Son mountains stretch over 700 miles along the western border. Northern Vietnam is mounainous except for the Red River valley. Southern Vietnam is relatively flat, drained by the Mekong River and tributaries.

There are two major rivers in Vietnam. The Mekong begins in eastern Tibet and flows 2800 miles to the South China Sea. Several tributaries join the Mekong before the river splits into many branches (called the Cuu Long or nine dragons) in the Mekong delta. The river flows continuously thanks in part to the Ton Le Sap, a natural reservoir in Cambodia. This reservoir receives a tidal backflow from the Mekong which is reversed as the Mekong level and flow decreases.

The other major river is the 250 mile long Red River. It begins in China's Yunnan province and discharges into the Gulf of Tonkin. Its major tributaries are the Lo (Clear) River, the Black River, and the Thai Binh River.

The climate is tropical monsoon with a single wet and dry season. Humidity stays about 70-80% with about 140 inches of rain. Temperature ranges from 62°F to 100°F in Hanoi and 78°F to 84°F in the south. The wet season is normally mid-May to mid-September with the cooler dry season the remainder of the year. This was an la Nina year with above average rainfall.

Cambodia is a somewhat circular country bounded on the east by Vietman, the north by Laos and by Thailand on the west and northwest. The central lowlands border Vietnam. There are three mountain ranges. Temperature ranges fro 24 to 32 C.

*****

History.

Vietnam's history stretches forward from the Lower Paleolithic (stone age) about 300,000 years back. Modern history embraces a succession of kings and invasions by the Chinese, Portugese, French, Japanese, and Americans. Details can be found in several books and on the internet.

Mesolithic sites near Hanoi date to between 5,000 and 3,000 BC. A bronze-age society developed by the Lac Viet on the Ma River called Dong Son. About 22 BC, the capitol was moved to Co Loa, 10 miles north of downtown Hanoi. This was captured by the Chinese who built a new provincial capitol at Luy Lau east of present day Hanoi.

Hanoi came into being as the capitol of the Ly Dynasty in 1010 AD at the end of the Chinese occupation. King Ly Thi To moved the capitol from Co Loa to where the To Lich River ran into the Hong (Red) River. It was called Thang Long or Dong Kinh. In the 19th centuary, the French corrupted Dong Kinh to Tong Kinh to Tonkin. The land was swampy delta land with numerous lakes and streams. A system of dikes surrounded the city marking the boundary. A fort overlooked the port of Dong Bo Dau. In 1902, the French consolidated their Asian colonies into the French Indochinese Union and chose Hanoi as its capitol.

The Japanese invaded in 1940 and set up a Vichy government to run the country. Ho Chi Minh siezed power in the 1945 August Revolution and proclaimed the independence of theDemocratic Republic of Vietnam. After WWII the French wanted to move back into the south while the Nationalist Chinese took the north. The French convinced China to leave and recognized North Vietnam independence. During the following eight years Ho Chi Minh's troops killed about 36,000 French troops culminating in the two month battle for Dien Bein Phu. Vietminh General Vo Nguyen Giap forced the surrender of 10,000 French soldiers. The Vietminh took the rest of North Vietnam and Laos. The dividing line was set near the 17th parallel along the Ben Hai River.

South Vietnam under Ngo Dinh Diem was supposed to have an election on reunification. The US backed Diem who declared himself President of the Republic of South Vietnam. The Vietminh (also called Vietcong) formed the National Liberation Front and began guerilla warfare in 1960. The modern history of the Vietnam war is readily available elsewhere.

The other major area we will visit in Vietnam is Ho Chi Minh City (formerly Saigon). Traders from India and China searched the coasts to find settllements and trading partners. Goods to and from India crossed the Bay of Bengal and were carried across the Isthmus of Kra then across the Gulf of Thailand to Saigon. From about 100 to 600 AD, this area was part of the Kingdom of Funan. From the last half of the 6th century it became part of the Khmer kingdom of Chenla (Zhenla). Beginning about 1,000 AD Saigon (called Gia Dinh Thanh), was a seaport controlled by the Angkor kingdom for about 200 years. In the 1500s, the Lac Viets invaded Cham and Khmer territory taking control of southern Vietnam until the French moved in.

Archeology and anthropology of Cambodia begins about 4,000 BC concluding about 800 AD. These were emerging stoneage people who began making contact with traders and missionaires from India and China. As the power of the Kingdom of Funan declined, the kingdom of Khmer/Zhenla expanded until 802 AD and the beginning of the Angkor or Kambuja Empire. The Angkor period ended in 1432 when the Thais sacked Angkor Thom. The capitol was moved to Phnom Penh.

*****

ANGKOR.

Since we will be flying to Siem Reap to visit the Angkor temple complex a short introduction seems appropriate. Siem Reap is about 200 miles northwest of Phnom Penh. The complex covers about 120 square miles and contains over 1000 temples. Many are collapsed or only a trace remains. The most famous structure is Angkor Wat.

The Angkor period covers the years between 802 to 1432. The area was occupied by the Chinese and Zhenla. The Angkor period extends from when the Zhenla emperor Jayavarman II established the Khmer empire until the Thais sacked the capitol of Angkor Thom in 1432.

The area was visited by traders and missionaries but Angkor was relatively unknown until a French naturalist visited in 1860. He died in 1861 and his diaries were published in 1864 describing the "lost city in the jungle" that were the work of ancient giant gods. In 1873 the French archeologist Louis Delaporte removed many of the best artifacts "for the cultural enrichment of France". In 1898 the French began clearing the jungle and mapping and restoring the site. This continued until 1930. In1953 the French and Cambodian joined in the Angkor Conservancy until 1970. In the mid-1980's Indian archeologists were contracted to clean and restore Angkor Wat causing more harm than good. UNESCO Commissioned the Japanese to develop a plan of action in 1989 with followup restoration contracts in 1991 when UNESCO commissioned Angkor as a World Heritage site. About a dozen sites are open for visitors.

Construction was out of wood, brick, latterite, and limestone. Kapok and fig tree roots have damaged many of the structures along with lichens and other vegetation. Lateritte is a soft stone that was easily carved when wet. It is sound when it dries but due to the humidity and clogging of the extensive system of ponds and canals the latterite has rehydrated and deteriorated.

There are books on the site, the art and the history of Angkor if you want more information.

The kingdom of Cambodia was a rural country, a former French colony (1863-1940). During WWII Thailand took control of western Cambodia and Japan siezed the remainder. The French regained control in 1945. The independent Kingdom of Cambodia was recognized in 1954. Cambodia tried to remain neutral but there were Vietnamese troops stationed in eastern Cambodia.

In 1970 General Lon Nol overthrew the prince and Cambodia was declared a republic. Nol attacked the Vietnamese and was defeated. The Cambodian communist (Khmer Rouge) antagonized the US who heavily bombed Cambodia. In 1975 the Khmer Rouge entered Phnom Penh under the leadership of Saloth Sar (better known as Pol Pot (political potential)).

Pol Pot tried to copy Mao by establishing a totally collecrive state where the entire population worked the land and the educated middle class was eliminated. In 1979 Vietnam invaded and eliminated the Khmer Rouge. During the four years 1.5 to 2 (1.7) million people died – a third of the population – from execution, torture, forced labor, disease, and starvation. Vietnam withdrew in 1989 and the monarchy was restored.

The killing fields monument and park was set up in Choeung Ek where 9,000 people were killed and buried. Pol Pot died of old age in 1997. Four other leaders, Nuon Chea, 85, chief ideologue of the Khmer movement; Khieu Samphan, 80, head of state; Ieng Sary, foreign minister; and Ieng Thirith, 79, minister of social affairs, were tried for genocide and other charges in 2011.

*****

Off and Running

Sunday, 23 Oct 2011. An e-mail arrived that we could check in and get boarding passes for tomorrows flight. It could not be done since this was an international flight.

Day 1. Monday, 24 Oct 2011. We left the house at 0545 by taxi to the San Antonio airport. We checked in at the Continental Airline counter. Check in with e-tickets was easy. We got boarding passes for the flights to Houston and Narita with bags checked to Hanoi. We would change to Japan Airline for the Narita to Hanoi leg.

We arrived in Houston about 0900 and found the international terminal about 1000. We boarded a 777 for the 16 hour flight to Narita near Tokyo, Japan. They provided two meals and a snack and supplied drinks about every hour. There were movies and music but I slept most of the way. There was a flight tracking map on tv that showed our track ran from south of the planned route. Houston to El Paso to Las Vegas to San Francisco across the Pacific to Japan arriving at 1420 Tuesday afternoon.

Carol left some stuff on the plane. This was retrieved before we went through immigration and customs.

We had arrived in terminal one and finally found our way to terminal two for check in and departure from Narita about 1800. The terminal was new and shiny. It had been built about 30 miles NE of Tokyo in a historic agricultural area after a lot of local resistance from famers and environmentalists.

We finally found Japan Airlines (JAL) and found that our bags were checked only to Japan. We found our bags and rechecked them to Hanoi. The route to Hanoi was SW over Tokyo to Nagoya to Fukuoka to Hangzhou to Guangzhou to Naning to Hanoi. Supper was oriental style food and included chopsticks. Nice looking efficient stewardesses. This was our first time flying JAL and I was favorably impressed after the Continental flight.

We arrived at Noi Bai International Airport serving Hanoi about 2100 hours on 25 Oct. This was a modern airport. Customs and immigration were painless. It was about 20°C (70°F), high humidity and no rain.

Our AMA tour guide met us and drove us through the dark about 28 km (30 minutes) to our hotel, the Metropole, in downtown Hanoi.

Traffic was heavy with cycles of all kinds, small cars, large Korean trucks, and tourist packed busses. Traffic passed on both sides and the wrong side of the road. Traffic flowed well at 20-30 mph.

After we checked in I bought $200 US in Vietnanese Dong at a rate of 21,000 per dollar. For the first time ever I became an instant millionaire.

While Carol was getting settled and ready for bed I went down for supper. Only thing open was the hotel bar. I ordered a prawn pizza and a Bai Ha Noi beer. The beer was good but the prawns on the thin crust pizza still had the shells on. The bar played the same music video repeatedly for the twenty minutes I was there.

It is always amazing that it takes about three days heading west and one day returning east crossing the International Date Line. It is still twenty-one clockhours on an airplane. I'm getting too old for this temporal abuse.

Day 2. Wednesday, 26 Oct 2011. We went down looking for breakfast and found it in the orangerie in the courtyard near the pool. Congee with all the fixings. Eggs to order. White Dragon fruit, watermellon, pineapple, and papaya. Bread pudding with choclate chips. Sweet rolls that were not sweet by US standards.

Vegetation near the pool included Alamandas, wood rose, Ixoria, Pothos on sugar palms, Blue Morning Glory, Hibiscus, Camelia, and Travelers Trees. Birds were Mynas and Eurasian Tree Sparrows.

The tour group gathered about 0800 and was divided into three groups. One thing I noticed was that there was no group introduction.

Hanoi Street Scene

About 0830, we loaded onto pedicabs for a city tour. Glad I was not driving. Rome or New York at rush hour was nothing like this traffic. Scooters and other small cycles were the majority mixed with push carts, pedestrians, taxis, and occasional busses and trucks. Sometimes the driver pedaled. Other times he pushed. The tour took about half an hour the recommended tip was one dollar US (The basic fee was contracted by the tour company). The vendor shot a picture of each occupant in his pericab with a print for "one dolla, GI".

Sites along the way included French colonial architecture, a couple ATMs, a sidewalk barbershop, a kid cutting meat on the sidewalk, coffee shops where people sat on short plastic stools, vendors selling almost anything you could want, and a one-hour laundry for a dollar a kilo. There were numerous parks and memorials and several small lakes.

I saw Streak-Eared Bulbuls, Eurasian Tree Sparrows, and Spotted Doves near the Presidential Palace and a Black Drongo near the One-Pillar Pagoda.

Next tour was Ba Dinh Square, the Ho Chi Minh Mausoleum, the Presidential Palace and park, Ho Chi Minh's house, the One-Pillar Pagoda, the Temple of Literature, and the water puppet show. Interesting day.

There is a large parade ground across from the Citadel. Located on the west side the Mausoleum was opened in 1975. It was copied after Lenin's tomb. Ho was embalmed by the Russian, Dr. Debor. It took a year to complete.

To the north of the Palace is the former French gouvenor's residence currently used as the official visitor quarters. There is a large pond called Ho's fish pond. The House of Ho Chi Min is a former servants quarters where he lived

Ho Chi Minh Tomb

instead of in the Palace. The lake and grounds were well landscaped. Ornamentials included Ixoria, Oleander, Bonhinia, Kapok, Teak, Fishtail palm, and some tree with aerial roots like Cypress knees.

The One Pillar Pagoda (Chua Mot Cot) was built in 1094. It has been rebuilt several times on the same foundation. Its form represents the pure lotus blosum. There were several souvenier shops in the plaza selling water puppets, musical instruments, plus all the normal tourist items.

One-Pillar Pagoda

We passed but did not visit the Ho Chi Minh Museum.

The Temple of Literature (Van Mieu Pagoda) dedicated to Confusius was built in 1070 modeled after a temple in Shantung where Confusius was born. It is the largest temple in Hanoi. This was the historic site where the 35-day doctorial examinations to become Mandarins were administred. We entered the first gate. The grounds covered a couple acres with giant Banyan and other trees. There were a lot of bonsai trees in pots and topiary animals with a variety of invasive weeds like Ruellia. The grass looked like Bermudagrass. Through the next gate was a pond and a line of 53 stelae naming the 1306 successful candidates for mandarin between 1442 and 1779. Each stelae is mounted on a tortoise, the symbol of strength and longevity.

On the way out we met a group of school girls in traditional dresses.

Back at the hotel we had lunch. Carol ordered borchetta and a Coke. I order a local beer and a panini and got a beer and some tall, fizzy drink. They took back the fizzy drink. I cancelled the panini and ate half Carol's borchetta.

The afernoon tour included the water puppet theatre. According to Wikipedia, water puppetry (*Múa rối nước*, "puppets that dance on water") is a tradition that dates back as far as the 11th century when it originated in the villages of the Red River Delta area of northern Vietnam. Vietnamese water puppetry is a variation on the ancient Asian puppet tradition of puppets carved out of wood then lacquered. The shows are performed in a waist-deep pool. A large rod supports the puppet under the water and used by the puppeteers normally hidden behind a screen to control the puppets. This makes the puppets appear to be moving over the water. This originated when the rice fields would flood and the villagers would entertain each other using this form of puppet play.

Water Puppet Theatre

The water puppet show played to sell-out crowds. Entertaining half-hour show. Reserved seating only.

After the puppet show we went to a market. Interesting. Live fish, snakes, and ducks, clothing, watches, etc.

Street Market

Back at the room the temperature had been turned down to 16°C (about 60°F). These hotels seem to think a duvet alone is a bed cover. At least this one was wider than the mattress. I prefer a sheet and a blanket if necessary.

I turned the heat up and we went for a walk. We hit a several art galleries and had dinner at the Opera House. Really good French cuisine.

Back at the hotel we repacked for the trip to Ha Long Bay.

Day 3. Thursday, 27 Oct 2011. We checked out and set the bags out to be loaded on the bus. After breakfast we boarded a bus for the four hour trip to Ha Long Bay in the Gulf of Tonkin. This is a UNESCO World Heritage Site and nominated as a modern wonder of the world.

We crossed the Red River. There were rice fields. duck farms, and ponds of lotus and water morning glory.

Most of the houses had a lotus symbol in the ridgeline center and the Buddist cobras (Naga) on the house corners. Many of the houses were about 20 feet wide 40 feet long and four stories tall. They say land, at $2,000 a square meter, is expensive, but up is free. An average 65 m² house runs about $150,000 so upwards is definitely cheaper. There is often a business in the ground floor and it looked like zero lot line zoning.

About two hours down the road we made a pit stop at a craft center. They made and sold laquer items, paintings, stone works, silk, etc. High quality and relatively low prices. Surface shipping was recommended and took about three weeks.

Craft Center

Highway 5 running from Saigon to the China border lead through rice fields that had been bombed during the war leaving pot holes everywhere. The yellowing heads of rice were being harvested by hand. Barn Swallows flitted through the humid air. A Great Egret waded in a canal. Depressions from bomb craters were common

Traffic was heavy. It seemed that our bus spent half the trip on the wrong side of the road tooting to pass cycles and other busses. Speed limit was 40 mph.

Cycles carried pigs, chickens, bags of rice, bundles of hay, and up to three or four people. Cyclists were required to wear helmets but many of the cheap plastic helmets were worthless and for looks only. There were few big cars or large mororcycles. Gas was about $4 a gallon. The little cycles got about 30-40 miles a gallon while cars and big motorcycles got about 20 and the trucks and busses much less.

We passed many tombs scattered in the fields. The tombs were sited using feng shui. Rice was planted around them and harvested like normal. Our guide discussed this. The dead were buried for about 2.5 years. Then one of the children or grandchildren would then clean the bones. These would then be dressed up in finery and placed in the tombs. We passed several areas where the tombs had been relocated in small areas to allow for factories and other public facilities. Fung Shui was ignored.

We passed through a range of hills that were being mined and the turn off to Haiphong that had been heavily bombed during the war.

We arrived at Bai Chay for lunch and then boarded a motorized wooden junk for an over night tour of the bay. A fancy bridge built by China connected Bai Chay to Hon Gai and continued the highway into China.

The bay had a low chop and no wind. Water had a tan cast due to the recent storm runoff. We sailed for a couple hours past colorful sea stack islands with sparse vegetation.

Our first stop was at Tiptop Island, a high island where a set of stairs had been installed to get to the top of the 300 foot peak for the spectacular view. I made the first hundred steps and decided with the overcast the rest of the climb was not be

Ha Long Bay

worth the effort.

Back on the beach I walked along the waterline and found a few oyster spat, some juvenile hard clams and a few small pieces of broken coral (Porites porites). This was a narrow beach of tan calcareous sand.

Several individual Ospreys cruised the sky. What appeared to be a few white gulls or terns were also seen but too far to identify.

With a low sun, the junk dropped anchor near the Cua Van floating village (one of four floating villages). This congregation of about 300 house boats and 600 people was anchored or moored around a small cove. The village could be moved to safety in case of a typhoon. Generations had lived on these boats fishing and pearl farming. Facilities included a government school and a doctor. There was bar and several shops all located on boats. A couple of boats had a generator and TV. There were numerous small boats for aquatic business.

We took a boat to the village where we changed to a skiff rowed by a woman standing and using two oars. Kids in boats dropped by selling stuff. Kids had their own boats and one kid was showing off rowing with his feet. By the time we returned to the dock it was dark.

Cua Van Flating Village

We returned to the ship for supper. There was food carving demonstration before dinner and folk songs and dance after supper.

We arrived at the Luon Bo anchorage for the night and dropped anchor. About 2200 I crashed.

Day 4. Friday, 28 Oct 2011. Good old jet lag. I was awake about 0200 and went up on deck to watch the clouds drift by. The constellation Orion was rising overhead. I sat in the breeze listening to the creaks of the ship's planks, the halyards beating on the masts and the rustle of the Vietnamese flag.

About sun rise, the Junk hoisted anchor and and probably woke everone. She headed to another floating community for a tour of the Cave of Surprises (Sung Sot Cave).

It was overcast and it just got light with no particular sunrise. Several Ospreys cruised the peaks of the islands. After tai chi and breakfast we boarded lighters for the trip to the dock. There was no beach and the catwalk met the rock about 20 feet above the water. There was big sign promoting the selection of Ha Long Bay to the modern Seven Wonders.

Ha Long Bay

We climbed about a hundred steps to the cave entrance. The cave was a dead cave. It had been dry for many years and the human impact had been considerable. A trail had been laid out through empty pools and dead stalactite formations with exotic names. The looping tour took about 45 minutes.

There were gift shops in the cave entrance and exit and on the docks. A few shells were on sale like a Tiger Cowry for $2 and $8 for a small Murex.

Back aboard the junk we repacked and set out the bags before going to brunch.

We were back ashore near noon and had time for a Coke while our bags were loaded on the bus trip to the airport for the flight to Siem Reap. A light rain began.

Most of the houses had some blue on them – trim, cornice, roof, walls. Both new and faded. I asked the significance and was told this had no significance except it was cheap and longlasting. Blue is a lucky color in the Middle East.

We stopped for lunch at a large golf resort. Lunch was nothing to brag about. The golf course was well designed and looked challenging. Landscape trees included tropical almond, papaya, alamanda, ixoria, and Jackfruit. Golfers were rich locals, Chinese, Japanese, and other orientals. There were several groups playing in the rain and more waiting to tee up.

The flight on Vietnam Airlines 737 was smooth. Our route crossed northern Vietnam, central Laos, and the eastern tip of Thailand before landing at Siem Reap in western Cambodia.

We landed after dark and were taken to our hotel/golf resort. After we found our rooms we hit the buffet for supper. Very good selection of local food and fruits. An Aspara show of native dance and music finished the evening.

Songs of two species of frogs seranaded us as we crossed the bridge over the pond leading back to our room.

Day 5. Saturday 29 Oct 2011. I woke as the sun was rising through the palm trees to the calls of Crested Mynah birds.

Breakfast was outstanding. Fruit new to me were the red Dragon fruit (<u>Hylocereus</u> <u>undatus</u>). The red Dragon Fruit was more tart then the white (<u>Selenacereus</u> <u>megalantherus</u>). Strange. Dragon Fruit is a cactus fruit raised in Vietnam and Malasia. It is native to Central America and called pitahaya in Mexico. I saw it near Oaxaca in Mexico. Lots of fresh French pastry or baguettes (*Noom paing* in Khmer). Good stuff.

About 0830 we gathered in the lobby for transportation to the Angkor World Heritage site. I saw a purple heron in a rice field ditch and a kingfisher flitting in brush along a major canal. I noticed that most of the buildings had one or more lightning rods installed. I asked about the lightning rods and was told lightning was common during the monsoon season.

We stopped at the South Gate for our three-day passes. There were hibiscus, Ixoria and various palms. Weeds included Bidens, Oxalis and

Anghor Thom

others invasive weeds. There were tiny purple or blue flowers like Houstonia and some thorny legume shrubs that looked like Neptunia and a purle flowered Dayflower. Large white and large yellow butterflies flitted in the distance. The road led through forest that included the big kapok and teak trees to Bayon then up the road by the terrace of the Leper King and the elephant terrace. A vendor was providing elephant rides. We visited Angkor Thom and then Bayon and the Ta Prohm temple. Details are available in numerous references,

Banyan trees were tearing up some of the sites and being constantly eliminated. Long-tailed Parakeets were calling and visible in the trees.

Like many other sites world-wide, there were numerous tours from many countries conducted in many languages. There were a few monks in orangish safron robes.

We returned to the hotel. Carol and I took a motorcycle cab called a tuk tuk to downtown for lunch. Lots of shops and tourists. Carol picked a resturant called "Viva" that specialzed in Mexican and Khmer foods. Carol had a burger and I had one of the fish local specialties. While we were eating a young man with both arms amputated asked if we would like to buy a book on Angkor. I looked at it and decided to suppliment

my other Angkor guide. He told us he lost his arms to land mines. Several mines had been planted by French, American, Khmer Rouge, Thai and Vietnamese for every person in the country over the past 50 years. I also bought a tee shirt to support the group that was sponsoring

Temple Bantey Srei

amputees education to work and not to beg, I asked if he had some post cards. He left and returned in a few minutes and I bought several packs of cards showing the Angkor sites. Another tuk tuk took us back to the hotel

About 1430 we left to visit the Bantey Srei temple and were caught in a shower. This was a small temple had some unique features.

Returning towards the hotel we stopped at a village to see palm sugar being made. They used sugar palms not coconut palms. The necter was boiled down a couple hours then poured into molds to set. The sugar drops were wrapped in palm leaf ready for sale. This village had other things for sale including scarfs and coconut crafts and woven palm leaf items. They had a large coconut tea pot, the first I had seen in years (I have a small one about 50 years old).

Palm Sugar making

It was about sunset when we stopped at the AMA school. The company sponsored an orphanage where dance, music and art was taught. The kids sang and danced for us and we shopped their crafts. I bought a good watercolor. It was rolled and slipped into a woven palm leaf tube.

So far it looks like the kids of Vietnam and Cambodia are different. Cambodiam kids are friendly and all over while the Vietnamese kids were more withdrawn. Many Cambodians act like we are entertaining them.

Back at the hotel it was time for a shower and another good supper. We went to the night market where I tried amok, a fish-based coconut curry served in a banana leaf packet. This is called the national dish of Cambodia and a home cooked dish in Thailand. It was very good.

We sat on a bench along the bridge in the middle of the lake and listened to the frogs and night sounds as the crescent moon rose. No mosquitoes but there were lots of leafhoppers around the security lights.

Day 6. Sunday, 30 Oct 2011. I was up for the sunrise. There were calls of the mynah birds and doves or pigeons in the distance. One tree frog was still chirping. Two men in a boat were trimming the floating vegetation along the edge of the lake.

After breakfast we loaded on the busses for the visit to Angkor. Along the railing of the causeways across the two moats were many Nagas (multihead cobras). Inside the walls there were banyan tree seedlings on the roof and ledges that are removed every year.

I went to the top (third level) of the major temple. On the way I saw a skink that disappeared into the rubble. Back on the ground there were some Plantago growing in the cracks.

Carol thought the walk would be too long and did not want to climb so she took a tuk tuk tour of the site.

Angkor Wat

We were back at the hotel for lunch and free time. Siem Reap was much smaller, guieter, and less hurried than Hanoi. There was traffic but not the jams of Hanoi. Since this was a tourist area and had only been developed over the past ten years the shops and resturants were much more modern and much cleaner.

We went shopping in the afternoon. One of the shops sold carved stone. I had been told of the replicas in Thailand that were sold as "instant antiques". The carver sat on the floor with the stone between his feet using mostly hand tools. He had a dust mask but no eye protection.

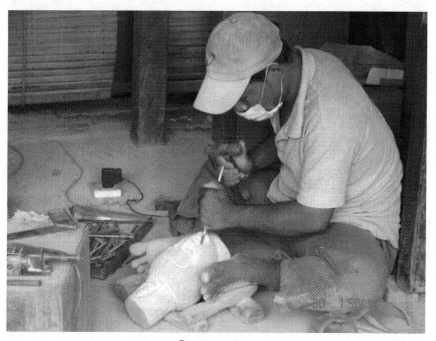

Stone carver

We repacked the bags and I crashed for a couple hours. About sundown we went downtown for supper and to visit the night market. The market was about two blocks long with jewelry shops instead of stalls, massage parlors, large aquariums for a fish pedicure, art galleries and several resturants. We bought two oil paintings that were demounted, rolled and put into a woven palm leaf tube. There were two foot massage places where you let fish do the work. Probably not too sanitary.

Supper was pretty good. I had banana blossom salad and another amok. Carol had beef and peppers that wassss not very spicy. We were the only ones in the resturant except the owner and his family. The little kids came up to the table several times to say hello and grin.

Night Market

At night there were flashing lights of the KTVs (Karoke bars). Our guide explained that these bars were often fronts for brothels and that many of the girls were under age. I later found that an NGO called Agape International Mission was trying to save these young girls that had often been sold to reduce family debt. Virgins were worth maybe $1500 to a brothel owner who then sold the girls to foreign pedifiles for $5,000 and up. Without a certificate of virginity young girls were only worth about $500 to the family.

Day 7. Monday, 31 Oct 2011. I was up about 0530 and finished packing and set my bag out. While Carol finished packing I went down to check out. After breakfast we loaded the busses and headed to meet the ship at Kampong Cham. I was disappointed to find we would not traverse Tongle Sap Lake with its birds, a hundred species of fish and unique vegetation. This was the time if year that the fish were stranded in the forest.

One of the Crested Mynahs was sounding like a Mocking bird with a variety of songs.

High water

The Tongle Sap Lake was still 10-15 feet high from the flood and monsoon water so we had to drive around the lake. The lake was about twice as large as usual and the water was still draining from the countryside flowing at maybe 4 kts.

The highway bypassed Tongle Sap Lake on the north and east, This was mostly rice farms.

There was still standing water on both sides of the road but water had covered the road a couple weeks previous.

About half way we passed through some hills with rubber plantations.

There were crops of casava and sugarcane, coconuts and bananas, and a tall grass grown for hay along with plots of corn and sweet potato.

The International Wildlife Federation was concerned about the loss of wildlife habitat due to the purchase of the open areas for agriculture.

After travelling about 200 km and three hours we came to the Mekong River at Kampong Cham about 1300. Our home for the next week, the RV La Marguerite, was moored to a muddy bank where the water had receded about 15 feet. The path to the ship was covered in sandbags to keep everyone out of the soft gray mud. We boarded and had lunch.

The rooms were soon ready and we were scheduled for a safety briefing at 1700 (bring your lifevest). The welcome dinner was at 1900 followed by a piano bar.

RV La Marguerite

Day 8. Tuesday, 1 Nov 2011. I was up 0530 before light and went topside to hang the sun up a little after 0600.

After breakfast we met about 0800 for a walking tour of Kampong Cham and the Dei Dos Pagoda.

The water was a thick coffee latte color too thick to drink but too thin to plow. The river was still dropping from the recent typhoon.

Various ships passed by – cargo types, ferries and fishing boats. I noticed some kids fishing and catching small catfish (Clarius batrachus?). The floodplain was almost totally scoured of vegetation and covered in silt. Further along the river men were setting out gardens of morningglory, casava, long bean, bitter melon, etc.

The first tour was to a pagoda. We walked about a half mile along the bund. Long thin fishing boats with long shafted outboard motors were beached. Fish traps were on the beach or protruding from the water. People were gathered talking, doing tai chi, sitting in outdoor coffee shops. We passed a small market with food and quart jars of scooter fuel. A fortune teller sat under a tree doing a fair business. There were several portable presses for making sugarcane or other juices. The asphalt street had quite a bit of traffic for the time of day.

Yellow Cassia shrubs ("yellow flower?") grew along the street. Other trees included Mango, African Tulip Trees, Jack fruit, and tropical almond.

There were a few tall Mast Trees with long crenate leaves.

On the beach people were fishing with poles, dip nets, gill nets, and cast nets. This was the fishing season with many fish having been swept down stream. The most popular were small catfish locally called Trey Dang Dau.

Along the inland side of the street were numerous small shops, several furniture factories, a coffin factory, a Catholic school, and numerous small coffee shops.

We entered the pagoda grounds and were greeted with a number of bell-shaped structures and a row of family tombs. The grounds were landscaped but not well maintained. I saw patches of Neptunia, morningglory, Bidens, Nightshade, Ruellia, Purslane, and knotweed. Poinciana trees, roses and camelias were in bloom.

Pagoda

Fishing Boat   **Garden Plots**

One of the large statues was a skinny golden budda. The temples were gold color with red tile roofs. There were a lot of gold colored life-size statues of Khmer figures like the elephant god and large Nagas on the stair hand rails.

Headed back to the ship we met several kids trying to fly home-made kites. Not much luck in the still, moist air.

About 0915 the ship cast off and steamed under the Mekong bridge. We arrived at Chong Koh a little after 1500.

We passed the town's large gold pagoda. The ship warped its way to dock at a small concrete pier. All of the kids in town and most of the adults met the boat with a friendly "Hello". Mats were laid out with silk goods for sale. Most of the group wanted to wait until we returned to make purchases but we picked up an escort of kids.

Chong Koh

The houses were all raised on piles with living areas under the houses. Smudge fires are often built under the houses to run the mosquitoes out. The yards were full of cycles, cows, and gardens and all the houses had a family shrine near the road. Several of the houses had looms set up under the houses producing silk scarves, table cloths and table runners.

One of the crops was black pepper. It grows on a vine. The leaf can be used with quid of a betel nut off the local palm trees and slaked lime to form a mild narcotic that stains teeth black and produces a red saliva. Lime and fish bones are sources of calcium. Anyway, the pepper berries are picked green for immediate use or sun dried to make black pepper or the husk of the dry pepper is removed to make white pepper. I did not see any stained teeth although betel nut is sometimes given to the kids to keep them quiet.

We looked at looms under a couple houses then went to visit a pagoda. If you judge the prosperity of the surrounding area by the looks and condition of the pagoda then Chong Koh was pretty well off. Well maintained and lots of gold leaf.

Back at the landing wheeling and dealing was underway. I bought several scarves and Carol bought a tablecloth, several scarves or *kramas,* and table runner.

This was a two hour stop. The ship cast off about 1730 heading for Phnom Penh.

So far the population looked healthy. Other than the amputees in Seim Reap there were no obvious invalids or skin or eye problems.

Discussion of local history with our guides showed that the general population was largely uninformed about recent history and the Khmer Rouge in particular. Cambodia and Vietnam both require schooling through grade 8 but many, particularly girls, don't get this far. School is in morning and afternoon with a siesta break. Many of the students get two years English. Many of the little kids say "Hello", "How are you", "How old are you" (since there is a respect for elders), and similar phrases. They giggled when I tried Khmer or Vietnamese phrases.

Post-Khmer Rouge society has reasserted teachings of the *Chbap Srei (The New Girl Book).* This 17th centuary Khmer guide is a long narrative poem outlining the desired behavior of young women. It was taught in pre-revolution public schools. It is repressive and a factor in slowing the recovery of the country. As a result, in this relatively poor society education of males is common and preferable although women operate many small businesses. No equality for women.

Day 9. Wednesday, 2 Nov 2011. We had anchored mid-channel at Phnom Penh. About sunrise we warped up to dock at the Sosowath Quay.

Phnom Penh was founded in 1434. It was occupied by the Japanese in WWII and the entire town was evacuated by the Khmer Rouge in 1975. Since 1979 there has been a lot of modernization and development.

After breakfast we had a bus tour of downtown Phnom Penh including the Royal Palace, the Silver Pagoda, the Wat Phnom, and the National Museum. Much of the city was of French Colonial architecture.

The palace was a 15,000 sf structure painted saffron and trimmed in gold. No pictures were allowed and you had to remove your shoes.

The Silver Pagoda and the National Museum had religious and historical artifacts many of which were gold or silver.

Just before returning to the ship we visited the Central Market. The market was busy but not crowded. It was somewhat divided as to type of merchandise, i.e. clothing, jewelry, etc. Everyone laughed when I bought a suitcase the haul all our loot.

After lunch we left at 1430 to visit the Killing Fields and Tuol Sleng (S21). The Killing Fields is located 15 km south of downtown at Choeung Ek. The road was lined with small shops and houses with flooded rice fields behind them.

The Killing Fields was a mass burial site where 8985 people had been mostly bludgeoned to death. A glass memorial stupa filled with skulls found nearby is the centerpiece. We walked through the park avoiding the excavated burial pits. There are interpretive signs throughout in English and Khmer theroughout the park.

Memorial Stupa   **Killing Fields excavations**

Returning to south Phnom Penh we stopped to visit the Tuol Sleng (S-21) Museum. This was the site of the former Tuol Svay Prey High School. It was modified to serve as a Khmer Rouge interrogation and torture center. At least 14,000 men, women, and children were processed and the majority were executed. Here were the offices of the secret department S-21.

S-21   **Torture Cells**

A Khmer childrens dance group performed after supper.

The ship spent the night tied up at the Quay. Some of the group went out for the evening to see the new Phnom Penh night life.

To the south about 150 miles on the Gulf of Thailand is the port of Kampot where weapons and war material were imported and sent up the Ho Chi Minh trail for use in the war. This port is on the Cambodia/Vietnam border.

I discussed the Tongle Sap lake and river and the Mekong with our guide. The Tongle Sap system serves as a safety valve by taking the overflow from the Mekong floods and releasing the water back as the Mekong drops. This anual pulse of water level provides irrigation and silt to be used for farming and stimulates the production of fish. Much of the fishery on the Mekong results from fish moved down stream. The decreasing number of large brood fish indicate a severe over fishing problem and an increased level of conservation and commercial fish hatcheriesis needed.

There are plans to construct about 50 dams along the Mekong in China and Laos the provide electrical power. Besides the loss of whole villages, agriccultural and forest areas the will be a drastic reduction in fishery production.

Day 10. Thursday, 3 Nov 2011. It was a colorful sunrise. My stomach was a little tender probably do to acidosis from eating too much fresh fruit. An Imodium tablet solved the problem.

Fishermen

There were a couple fishermen using cast nets. They were catching fish and taking a swim if they slipped on the steep concrete wall.

After breakfast we boarded busses for a 20 mile ride to Oudong. There were rice fields and several small villages along the road. A flock of white egrets occupied one rice field. There were several fish farms along the road.

Fish Farm

Oudong became capitol of the Khmer Empire in 1618. King Norodom moved the capitol back to Phnom Penh in 1865. Much of the city was destroyed by air strikes on the Khmer Rouge that occupied the city in the 1970s.

Entering Oudong I saw a cell phone shop and a pharmacy then a resturant then another phone shop and pharmacy. There were half a dozen phone shops and seveal pharmacies along about a mile of street.

Come to think of it along the river we were seldom out if sight of a cell tower.

The road lead to the Buddhist Monastery of Vipassana Dhura the largest monastery in Cambodia. There were about 50 monks in residence. We walked around the grounds and went to the main building for the monks blessing. After this we visited a large building with many Bhuddist style paintings.

I looked at the grounds and pond. They were landscaped with ornamental shrubs and flowers and statues of Khmer mythology and well maintained.

Buddhist Monastery of Vipassana Dhura

There was some construction going on. I saw a welder welding without eye protection and watched a man about three stories up installing roofing materials without shoes or a safety line. I guess only the materials had changed in the past thousand years. Like the stone cutter in Siem Reap that held the stone between his feet while he hammered a chisel with a dust mask but no eye protedtion. OSHA would have a fit.

Forty-five minutes down the road was Kampong Tralach. This was a small farming community where we had a short ride in an ox cart. The ride was through the village where all the kids turned out to wave and holler "Hello". Some of the kids were selling wild flowers. It is important that they were selling something and not begging.

Ox carts are important in some rural areas used similar to a truck to haul food, feed, and materials. The ox is used in dry area and the water buffalo in used where it is much wetter.

Ox Cart Ride

We returned to the ship for a free afternoon. Carol wanted to go shopping so we found a tuk tuk that took us to a shop that sold good jewelry and antiques. She spent a half hour looking and bought a scarf while our tuk tuk waited. Then he took us to another shop for jewelry and then to the Russian Market and finally to the older Central Market

(*Pasa Tamey*). I bought three pairs of Levi's 560 cargo pants for $10 each and a couple five dollar T-shirts. (I later found the pants had flaws but they are good work pants.) They do not match anything currently shown on the Levi's website. About two hours in our tuktuk cost ten bucks. The driver may have also received a percentage of everything we bought. If this is like Thailand and many other countries the bigger stores each own a fleet of tuktuks and drivers.

There was a Khmer music and dance show by local musicians on board after supper. The folk songs and music mostly represented rural life.

Out on the deck gekos hiding in the potted plants were calling. A low pressure front had rolled in from the southwest and the evening sky was filled with heat lightning. Lightning flashes appeared outlining the clouds but there was no thunder. Heat lightning lit up the eastern sky backlighting tall sugar palms and cell phone towers.

Day 11. Friday, 4 Nov 2011. After midnight it rained for about an hour. The morning came up breezy and cooler.

I was on deck with a pot of tea about 0600 waiting for the sunrise and watching the river traffic and the city come alive. The guys with castnets were at work. Big clumps of water hyacinth were floating down stream in the tan flood water.

We left the quay and headed east 120 km for the border crossing into Vietnam near Tan Chau. The river banks were punctuated with houses, small villages and factories. The horizon was scalloped with scattered tall teak or kapok trees and sugar palms. A few barge trains were carrying sand from river dredging sites.

The sky was a white overcast like the monsoon was back. Lightning was back for the evening.

We anchored midstream for the customs check. Skiffs with officials arrived at both sides and left after about two hours. During this time the crew held classes on folding napkins and towels and fruit sculpting and the chef demonstrated how to make fresh spring rolls.

Villages and Fish Traps

Several of us watched fishermen setting hoop nets and using castnets from boats in the shallow water. There were also large permanent traps.

The ship pulled the hook and we continued about 25 km to our Tan Chau anchorage. During this period there was an ice cream party.

There was a briefing for tomorrow's tours followed by supper. This was my birthday and I was surprised when the cookstaff brought out a birthday cake and sang "Happy Birthday". We consumed about a third at our table and I walked around to each of the other tables offering birthday cake. Supper was followed by a crew talent show of songs and folk dances and then by karyoki music for dancing. I went up on deck to watch the lightning show for a few minutes before crashing.

Monsoon sunset on the Mekong

Day 12. Saturday, 5 Nov 2011. About 0600 the sun crawled out of a cloud bank like the low pressure front had passed.

The excursion process is pretty orderly. The group is split into three groups of about 20 and each group is designated by a color. We were in the yellow/orange group. Each person had a boarding card that you picked up on leaving the ship and turned in when you returned so they could keep track of people. Pretty efficient.

We left the ship at Tan Chau and were picked up by bicycle rickshaws (tuktuks), one person per, much like we had in Hanoi. They pedaled and pushed until we reached a silk factory where they made many silk items. A single weaver on a loom could produce about 5 meters of silk a day. The new machinery can do about 25 meters a day and a single person can maintain 5 to 6 machines. I bought Carol a colorful silk dress after asking several tour women if they thought it would fit and some more *kramas*.

Next was to the boat landing. We loaded aboard a small passenger boat and headed out to see the floating fish farms and a small island village. "Put on your life preservers".

Pedirickshaws (tuk tuk)   **Silk factory**

The floating fish farms were metal barges with wire mesh cages hung from the deck. The cages were 7X15X2 m (25 by 50 feet and six feet deep) wire mesh covered with chain link. The fish were fed commercial fishfood 1.5% protein. Fingerlings are purchased and fed out. The catfish sold for about a buck a kilo. The choice fish was the Red Tilapia that brought $1.50-$2.00 per kilo. Construction cost per unit was about $50,000. It would have been interesting to see more than ten minutes of the process. Much of the world has problems with cage culture because the local river current is not enough to remove the waste away from the cages. If the Mekong flows like this all the time they are lucky to keep the cages from floating away. The Mekong is 50 to 120 feet deep and is running 2-3 knot current.

Floating Fish Farm   **Fish Cage**

Tree sparows were living in the eves and feeding on the fish food. Heading back I saw several gulls and a couple white terns.

Next stop was a village on the island. Crops included millet, melons, corn, and rice. Kids all over. The village had about 600 people. They also harvested pepper and pepper leaf, Jackfruit, mangoes, taro, and long beans. They also produced tea seedlings. There was a couple trays of fish drying in the sun.

Small Farm

Birds included egrets, a crow, and miscellaneous small birds.

We returned in time for lunch. After lunch our guides held a question and answer session about Cambodia and Vietnam. Interesting to hear their ideas and impressions.

About 1830 there was a briefing on tomorrow's tour followed by supper. We pulled the hook and headed down stream for Sa Dec. Nice evening to sit on deck in the dark and watch the lightning. It rained for a couple hours in the middle of the night.

Day 13. Sunday, 6 Nov 2011. We were anchored midstream on a cool, breezy morning. The sun did not come up, but the swallows were busy over the river.

The day's tour was to Sa Dec, a busy port and industrial center. During th Vietnam war this was the headquarters for some US Swift boats and later some of the A boats.

This was the home of Marguerite Duras between 1928 and 1932. Her mother ran a school. Duras had an affair with Huynh Thuy Le that became the basis for Duras' 1984 prize winning novel, "The Lover". She was the namesake of our ship.

After breakfast we boarded local boats for a ride across the river and up one of the small tributaries. We passed boat yards, houses and numerous shops overlooking the water including a coffin factory.

We stopped to visit a brick factory. They import the clay and sand and mix it at the factory. Much of this material comes from dredging the river channel. The bricks are formed up and allowed to sun dry for a day. Then 10,000 bricks are loaded in a kiln and cooked for 30 days using rice husk for fuel. After the bricks are loaded and the fire lit the wall of the kiln is bricked shut. The sale price was 30 bricks for a dollar. Since there are 525 bricks to a bundle or pallet this would be about $17.50. Local price for similar bricks in San Antonio, Texas, ran about $425.

Living on the Mekong

Floating Market

Coffin Maker

Next stop was downtown to visit. We disembarked at a quay along the main street. The inland side of the street had all kinds of shops. The the Lover's Museum was the house that was the home of her lover and where Duras's book was located. Green tea and cookies. Her mother's home and school are still in use as a school. There were pictures of the writer and the stars who acted in the movie adaptation.

We visited the Fujian Temple next door. This was donated to the city by the Le family.

Cai Be Waterfront and Catholic Church

After Church

Market   **Candy Factory**

After lunch we took a boat to Cai Be. It has a large floating market where boat loads of produce is sold wholesale. Boats loaded with lechees and other produce anchored and opened for business. There were also shops along both banks.

We stopped down town to visit the street market. At the quay we crossed the street to visit a Franciscan Catholic church with two large grotoes lining the side yards. A group of students were taking a break after services, the girls in long white dresses and the boys in black pants and white shirts. There was also had a couple cages with a howler monkey, a macaque, and a couple apes.

The market had vegetables, fruit, meat, and live fish, eels, frogs, turtles, and ducks. All this on both sides of the street with cycle traffic running down the middle.

We took a walk to a shop where sleeping mats and slippers were made. The straw was dyed and then woven by machine. Next we visited a candy factory where they made coconut candy, edible rice paper, sweet puffed rice, and other Asian candies. They also brewed local wines – rice, banana, sugar cane and one with a snake in it. We got to sample everything but I don't think anyone tried the snake. They also had a big selection of local crafts.

We headed towards the landing to catch our boat and one of the vendors was selling "'water coconut". I'm not sure but this looked and tasted like immature or green coconut.

Back on the ship we paid our bill and handed out the tips and prepared for the farewell dinner and a musical show. I sat out on the deck after supper watching the lightning, listening to a geko calling. Looking around, I saw several gekos near the light fixtures catching bugs.

Day 14. Monday, 7 Nov 2011. We pulled the hook about 0700 and sailed about 70 km to the port of My Tho. About 0830 we offloaded to busses for a sight seeing tour of Thanh Pho Ho Chi Minh (Ho Chi Minh City or old Saigon) on the way to the hotel.

The scattered farmland and small villages gradually became more complex. Finally, a wide street with business buildings. We stopped to view a Chinese Budist temple. Next stop was for a quick walking tour of the Notre Dame cathedral and the post office designed by Dr. Eiffel. The former US Embassy and CIA headquarters were pointed out.

Next was a quick trip through the central market.

Chinese Temple

We stopped for lunch at the five star *Indochin Resturant*. This took over an hour. We left the resturant for the hotel about 1400, check-in time.

Of all the places we hit on this trip all had modern Japanese Toto toilet fixtures except for one French bombsight. Even the smaller towns had running water. I'm sure this does not apply everywhere but our tour guides have really taken care of us. There are few public facilities so I never pass up one.

This was a five star hotel. We moved in and went out to look at a few art galleries and shops.

Central Saigon

Central Market

Sidewalk?

Central Post Office

About sundown we went to the hotel dining room. Carol got a decent burger and fries. I wanted to get a Mexican food fix and ordered quesadas. No bueno. The tortilla was replaced by flat bread; it had ground meat and no cheese; a really mild chili sauce; and yogurt in place of sour cream. Even their breakfasts dishes were hybridized Asian and European dishes. I guess the menu was for the upscale international visitors since they did not have much local food and everythig I saw had a chef's touch.

Old CIA Headquarters

Day 15. Tuesday, 8 Nov 2011. After breakfast we toured downtown including the Presidential Palace where we saw the ceremonial rooms and the private apartments with its heliport, then down to the basement and through the command post with the old teletype machines. A pair of Russian tanks that had invaded the Palace grounds were on display.

Presidential Palace

Seeing the various weapons on display reminded me of an engineer I knew who worked as a civilian in Saigon. Civilians were not permitted to have weapons of any kind but he always carried a pistol stuck in his waistband. I asked if he ever shot anyone and he just grinned. Another civilian worker said he was ashamed of the way Americans treated hired Vietnamese help. When he moved into government quarters the maid was expected to clean the toilets with a rag but no gloves, brushes, or chemicals. He procured a pair of rubber gloves for her.

Near the hotel we stopped at a lacquer factory where lacquerware was crafted. Pictures. Screens. Furniture. Containers. Really well done. Prices were very reasonable but the cost of shipping was prohibitive.

Artist

Setting the pattern

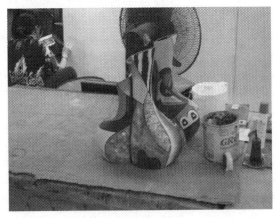

Art

Display

After lunch I took a tour that drove past Tan Son Nhat airport about twenty miles NW of HCMC under grey skies to see the 162 sq miles Cu Chi Tunnels park, aka by GIs as Hobo Woods.

We stopped to visit the Cu Chi National Cemetary containing about 10,000 graves. Lots of bodys were never found.

This whole situation came about in part from our brilliant strategy of pacification called Strategic Hamlets where a number of small farming villages were left alone. Instead of pacification this allowed the Viet Minh (VC) and the North Vietnamese Army between 1948 and 1973 to construct 217 miles of tunnels up to three levels as much as 50 feet deep containing bunkers, command posts, hospitals, etc, all underground. These were not discovered for over ten years. The area was full of booby traps and contained hundreds of troops. As a result of taming this area it has been described as "the most devastated, bombarded, defoliated and gassed in the whole history of warfare."

We had a briefing on Cu Chi including one of the old VC propagada movies and were led around the the area. One display was a tip-up trap with pungy sticks. There were US and Vietnames weapons and several of the facilities that had been opened up for view. Several bomb craters still evident.

Cu Chi Cemetary

The guide pointed out an air vent hidden in one of the numerous termite mounds. We were shown one of the bunkers and its hidden entrance holes. Tourists were allowed to enter. There was another 20 foot tunnel connecting two opened bunkers that we were allowed to crawl through. The guide said the tunnel had been enlarged and we could duckwalk through it. I'm afraid my days of duckwalking are over so I went through on my hands and knees.

Cu Chi Map   **Bunker Entrance**

Old Bomb Crater

During the war some of the tunnels were cleared by a group of soldiers called "Tunnel Rats". I met one of the Tunnel Rats. He had been weird before he spent a year crawling through these tunnels in the dark.

Although the area had been bombed on purpose it was also used as a dumping place for hung ordnance since planes could not land with bombs and rockets still attached.

There were two gift shops with T-shirts, etc. Nearby was a firing range where you could fire vintage weapons and a museum of planes, etc from the war era but we did not have enough time for these activities.

Next stop was a rubber plantation with taps collecting latex. Each tree had tap and a plastic collar to keep rain from diluting the latex. Latex is boiled or roasted to remove the water then shipped for further processing. Ford Motors had large plantations and, according to a speech by President Eisenhower, we fought the war to protect rubber and our other strategic materials coming from Vietnam. I guess all wars have their corporate sponsors. Shades of the Gulf Wars!

Rubber Tree Plantation

Rubber Collection

Many of the fields contained bomb craters that were slowly being filled. Many of the fields had ornate above ground tombs like we saw near Hanoi. There were nurseries for ornamental plants used around Saigon. They also raised thousands of young rubber trees for the plantations.

Back at the hotel we decided to go out for supper. We took a taxi to the *Hoi An* recommended by our tour director. Very good. I had the 8 course menu. Carol had egg rolls and lemon chicken. There was a three piece group playing local music on local instruments –a flute, a concave guitar and a strange one string instrument that sounded like a moog.

Old Saigon

Day 16. Wednesday, 9 Nov 2011. This was the last day but our flight did not leave until 2355. We paid for a late checkout so we could stay in the room and do some shopping.

After breakfast I went by myself to see the botanical garden and zoo. It was not bad for a small park with cages for common zoo animals. There were several small specialized gardens for palms, cactus, etc., and a small greenhouse. There was no book store and I found no books any where on plants and birds of Vietnam.

After I returned we hit a few more shops and a couple more galleries, returned to the hotel, and checked out about 1800. After checking the bags we went out for supper at the hotel recommended *Xu* resturant. It was pretty good but not nearly as good as the previous night.

A cab took us out to Tan Son Nhut about 2100. We had to wait an hour until the ticket counter opened. Our bags were checked to San Antonio and we headed for the gate. Through one passport check and body scanner then another passport check and body scanner and we were at the gate. Another half hour and we were on the plane for a four hour flight to Narita in Tokyo.

Day 17. Thursday, 10 Nov 2011. We arrived at Narita about 0630 local. Good thing there was a 10 hour layover because navigating to our next gate was not intuitively obvious unless, maybe, you were born there. Catch a train then go down three floors and catch a bus then try to find the right gate. Several people indicated, "that way". One young lady in a uniform said she had no idea. Finally, I asked a policeman who actually put us on the right path.

We got lunch at the terminal's McDonald's. High cost low quality Japanese copy of a burger and fries and a drink. Fifteen bucks each.

Carol checked into a $15 dollar an hour roomette for a couple hours sleep. These are handy for long layovers.

We stopped at the Hermes retail outlet. Carol checked on the price of a small purse similar to the knockoff she had bought in Saigon and found they were asking $2,700. I saw some ties for $175 each with $750 white dress shirts. Wow! I save almost a thousand dollars a day by being retired and not having to dress up. There were other outlets but one round of sticker shock was enough for me.

1700 Thursday finally arrived and we were on our way to Houston, 16 hours flying time across 9 time zones. We landed in Houston about 1700 for the second timethat day. After immigration and customs and rechecking the bag we were off to San Antonio about 1900. A taxi delivered us home about 2100 the same day.

After thought and Comments

Altogether, it was a good trip. AMA Waterways tour was a success. I did not get to see the Hanoi Hilton or the Ho Chi Minh trail but I did see the Angkor complex and the Killing Fields in Cambodia and the Tunnels at Cu Chi near Saigon.

Extras included Hanoi/Saigon traffic, seventeen new birds seen, many new plants such as the Mast Tree, fog and rain along the Mekong, heat lightning, fish farms, canals and jungle, agricultural practices, the recovery from Agent Orange, fields still pockmarked with bomb craters, and lots of other details.

It surprised me to see many of the signs in Vietnamese or Khmer with English subtitles and the preferred use of dollars. Even ATMs spit out dollars. I prefer to use dollars so I can compare the asking price with the price at home without mental gymnastics or a calculator.

I was somewhat surprised to see rebuilt modern cities and the development of the tourist trade. Hanoi, Saigon, and Phnom Penh with a mix of old and new were fascinating.

Vietnam belongs to the Trans-Pacific Partnership (TPP), the Pacific version of the NAFTA free trade agreement, along with the US and Australia so imports and exports are duty free. This was news to me.

It was interesting to see "factories" at work. These were a few hundred to a couple thousand square feet of open covered space with no walls. Ppeople or machines were turning out a variety of products from candy to clothing to furniture.

I suppose the war had some benefits. It removed over a million people from an overcrowded area. It also forced modernization of the cities, infrastructure and government.

I was in the US Naval Reserve during the Vietnam war and did not get drafted. My unit did participate in the Da Nang airlift twice but I was bumped from the crew in Hawaii both times.

After my pretrip research on the Vietnam, Cambodia and the Vietnam war, hearing comments from the Vietnamese and Cambodian side, being on site and seeing the areas of conflict were enlightening.

I have changed my mind about the leadership and conduct of the war. During US military indoctrination the Southeast Asian people were dehumanised, their God-given right to self-defence was delegitimised. Their resistance was reframed as terrorism and US soldiers were sent expressly to kill. This was nothing new. From an historical perspective Vietnam was a continuation of the WWII and Korean mindset.

Actually Vietnam was lucky. In 1954/5 under President Eisenhower an "A-Day" was proposed to make a permptive nuclear strike on the Communist world including Russia, China, and Korea. Thankfully this day never came. Eisenhower even offered to help France's plight by bombing Dien Bien Phu where France eventually lost possession of North Vietnam. France refused. In 1962 there was a proposal to nuke Laos to prevent Communist takeover.

I tend to agree with at least some of the war protestors that there was poor upper level leadership. The war was highly political and underwritten by big business. Basic training for both enlisted and officers stressed a subhuman enemy and the need to kill anything that moved. This was much like the war with Japan where Japan was seen with no civilians. Munitions and other war fighting equiptment was big business on all sides. Weapons were redesigned to maim and mutilate rather than outright killing

I did not agree with the poor treatment of the veterans by the US public. Our military were mostly professional and fought well considering their foggy orders and the political constraints. The proposed domino theory of Communist states was wrong. Communism was already a failed system and our leaders did not choose to have basic faith in democracy particularly when there was a economic potential. Our leaders alienated civilians and military alike to a point where you could have soon had a revolution brewing as Johnson and Nixon learned and events in Russia, Egypt, and Libya demonstrated. The Washington bureaucrats overrode the field commanders and demoralized the troops on the ground as well as the general population in the US. Targets were handpicked in Washington to avoid possible involvment by China or Russia.

The war in Vietnam killed many soldiers on both sides and numerous Vietmanese civilians. It also psychologically damaged many on both sides. Barbarism allowed the worst human traits to be demonstrated as new cases of PTSD are still being uncovered. Atrocities and barbarism during this war is documented in a new book by Nick Tergel titled, *Kill Anything that Moves*. At the height of the war our troops operated on the MGR (Mere Gook Rule) principle to dehumanize the enemy and calling them gooks, slopes, rice eaters, etc. Many US veterans brought back personal items scavaged from the ruins or taken off the dead, i.e, pictures, letters, etc. A few brought back trophies like ears.

Recently released recordings made in the Johnson Whitehouse indicate that the Johnson's presidential race was sabotaged by Nixon. Nixon had approached the Vietnamese suggesting they not attend the Paris peace talks until after the election which they did. He also told his billionaire's club friends that he would see to it the war would continue as long as possible. President Johnson threatened Nixon with treason but Nixon outsmarted the Johnson by getting on the Sunday morning talk shows and saying he was going to do all he could to stop the war thereby getting himself elected. Without Nixon the war might have ended earlier but then there would have been no Nixon visit to China. Can't win them all.

Birds

Pandionidae / Osprey

Osprey / Pandion haliaetus	Hanlon Bay

Ardeidae / Egrets

Purple Heron / Ardea purpurea	Siem Reap rice field
Great Egret / Egretta alba	Rice fields near Hanoai
Little Egret / Egretta garzetta	Small flocks
in rice fields along Mekong	

Laridae / Gulls and Terns

Little Tern / Aterna albifrons	Mekong Delta
Herring Gull / Larus argentatus	Mekong Delta

Alcedinidae/ Kingfishers

Common kingfisher / Alcedo atthis	Siem Reap

Psittacidae/Parrots

Long-tailed Parakeets / Psittacula longicauda	Anglor Thom

Columbidae/Doves

Spotted Dove / Streptopelia chinensis	Siem Reap and Phnom Penh

Hirundinidae/Swallows

Barn swallow / Hirundo rustica	Hanloh Bay, Mekong River

Pycnonotidae

Streak-Eared Bulbul / Pycnonotus blanfordi	Hanoi

Dicruridae

Black Drongo / Dicrurus macrocercus	Hanoi

Sturnidae

Common Myna / Acriditheres tristis	Hanoi
White-vented Myna / Acriditheres javanicus	Mekong Delta
Crested Myna / Acriditheres cristatellus	Siem Reap

Passeridae

Eurasian Tree Sparrow / Passer mintanus	All major towns

Corvidae

Racket-Tailed Treepie / Crypsieina temia	Mekong Delta

Fish

Catfish	Clarius batrachus ?	Mekong River
Cichlids	Tilapia sp	Mekong fish farms

Plants

Acanthaceae	Ruellia / Ruellia sp
Anacarsiaceae	Mango / Mangifera indica
Annonaceae	Mast tree, sorrowless tree / Polyathia longifolia pendula
Apocyanaceae	Olrander / Nerium oleander
	Frangipani / Plumeria obtusa
	Golden Trumpet / Allamanda cathartica
	Vinca / Vinca sp
Araceae	Taro / Colocasia esculenta
Bignoniaceae	African Tulip Tree / Spatheodea campanulata
Bombacaceae	Kapok Tree / Bombax ceiba
Bromeliaceae	Pineapple / Ananas comosus
Cactaceae	Yellow Dragon Fruit / Hyalocereus megalanthus
	Red Dragon Fruit / Hyalocereus undatus
Commelinaceae	Day flower / Commelina sp
Compositae	Wedelia / Wedelia trilobata
	Centurea sp.
Cruciferae	Rockets / Hesperis mattronalis
Cucurbidae	Bitter melon, Balsam Pear / Momordica charantia
	Watermelon / Citrullus vulgaris
Euphorbiaceae	Copperleaf / Acalypha sp
	Crown of Thorns / Euphorbia milii
	Cassava / Manihot esculenta
Graminae	Corn / Zia Maise
	Sugar cane / Sorgham vulgare var saccharatum
	Rice / Oryza sativa
Ipomea	Water Morning Glory / Ipomea aquaticus
Leguminosae	Bauhinia / Bauhinia purpurea
	Royal Poinciana / Delonix regia
	Yellow Flower / Cassia sp
	Sensitive Briar / Neptunia sp

	Long bean / <u>Vigna</u> <u>susquipedalis</u>
	Soy Bean / <u>Glycine</u> <u>max</u>
Leucocassia	Tsro / <u>Colocasia</u> <u>esculenta</u>
Liliaceae	Corn Plant / <u>Dracaena</u> <u>fragrans</u>
Musacaea	Banana / <u>Musa</u> sp
	Traveler's Tree / <u>Ravenala</u> <u>madagasgarensis</u>
Moraceae	Banyan Tree / <u>Ficus</u> <u>benghalensis</u>
	Rubber tree / <u>Ficus</u> <u>elastica</u>
	Jackfruit / <u>Artocarpus</u> <u>heterophyllus</u>
Nyctaginaceae	Bougainvillea / <u>Bougainvillea</u> <u>glabra</u>
Oxalidaceae	Oxalis / <u>Oxalis</u> sp
Palmaceae	Fishtail Palm / <u>Caryota</u> <u>mitis</u>
	Sugar Palm / <u>Arenga</u> <u>engleri</u>
Piperaceae	Knotweed / <u>Polygonum</u> sp
Plantaginaceae	Plantain / <u>Plantago</u> <u>Psyllum</u>
Ponrederiaceae	Water Hyacinth / <u>Echhornia</u> sp
Portulaceae	Purslane / <u>Portulaca</u> sp
Polyginaceae	Black Pepper / <u>Piper</u> <u>nigrum</u>
Rubiaceae	Ixora / <u>Ixora</u> <u>stricta</u>
	<u>Houstonia</u> sp ?
Sapindaceae	Leechee, Lyche, Litchi / <u>Nephelium</u> <u>Litchi</u>
Solanaceae	??
Teaceae	Tea / <u>Thea</u> <u>sinensis</u>
Urticaceae	Artillery Plant / <u>Pilea</u> <u>microphylla</u>
Verbenaceae	Teak / <u>Tectona</u> <u>grandis</u>
	Frob-bit / <u>Phyla</u> sp.

Notes

See Wikipedia on Ha Long Bay. References for plants and animals. Geologic history.

Hanoi

Angkor Wat

Ha Long Bay

Mast or Sorrowless Tree

Buddhist Monastery

Rush Hour in Saigon

Vietnam and Cambodia are growing into modern countries and probably no longer classed as third world. Their public health and tourist industry is thriving. We enjoyed the trip.
Carl

Poems
of
Cambodia and Vietnam
2011

Carl Lahser

Contents

Hạ Long Bay

Hạ Long Bay, Vietnam
Vịnh Ha Long
Bay of the Descending Dragons
The 2,000 emerald karst islets
Were spit out by protective dragons
And jewels and jade
Sprang up in front of enemy ships

Hạ Long – the place where mother dragon lived
Bái Tú Long – where lived her children
Islets swathed in a hundred kinds of trees
Protecting Haiphong
Protecting Vietnam

A quiet night on the Bay
Watching Scorpio overhead
Hearing halyards slapping the mast
Listening to the creaking wooden hull
Quiet and a pot of tea.

Carl 28Oct11

Water Puppets

In Hanoi live the water puppets
In a pool telling farmer's stories
Mounted on rods beneath the surface
Operated by puppeteers waist deep
Hidden artists and three foot actors
Carl26Oct11

Typhoons

Typhoons, teeth of the Southeast Asian gods
A storm one hundred thirty years ago
Hit the Gulf of Tonkin
Decimated Haiphong
Killing 300,000 in the Red River Valley

In April 2011 a storm hit Saigon
On24 September Typhoon Haitang hit Hanoi
On 30 September Typhoon Nesat hit Haiphong
On 9 Oct Typhoon Banyan hit Hong Kong
The Mekong rose 30 feet
And 3000 people were killed
Most of Thailand was flooded

Water will still be standing for months
Tong le Sap Lake was 70 miles wide
Quiet and humid
And a falling barometer
Need to listen to the weather man
It's coming.

Carl 10Oct11

Scooter Heaven

Southeast Asian streets
Hanoi, Saigon, Phnom Pehn
A writhing sea of
    Motor scooters,
    Motorbikes,
    Rickshaws,
    Pushcarts
    Cars,
    Busses
    Ox carts
    Old women with a loaded yokes

Crossing a street
Walking into traffic with your hand raised
Walking at a steady pace
While demons fly past
Emerging on the other side unscathed.
Wheee!
                Carl 26Oct11

Snack Time

Sidewalk cafes
With red or blue plastic chairs
And knee-high plastic tables

Serving tea and pho
Talking news
Telling jokes
Oblivious as the world flows past
Carl26Oct11

Sidewalk Market

Bok Choy
Dichon
Water morning glory
Taro roots
Peeled pineapples
Leeches
Rice
Sitting on the sidewalk
Resting on low tables
While the old women sit
Talking or dreaming of better days
Carl27Oct11

Fish Market

Crabs and eels
Catfish
Snails and turtles and frogs
It's all edible, Joe
I clean it for you, Joe
Right here on the sidewalk
30Oct11

Farm House

In a clearing off the road
Beyond the family shrine
Past the tethered water buffalo
And jackfruit trees
A house on stilts
With hammocks strung between the posts
A loom on one side
Lightning rods for the monsoon
A lotus and Nagas on the roof ridge
Thatch roof
Blue shutters
Waiting for the monsoon to slaken
Waiting for the Mekong to recede

Carl 31 Oct 11

Mekong River

A mile wide and fifty feet deep
The Mekong flows from China
Then between Laos, Vietnam, and Cambodia
Essential highway

Suddenly the halyards beat against the mast
Evening monsoon clouds slide in
Cool and loaded with rain
Sheet lightning highlights tall clouds
Humidity and rain fill the night

Overcast daylight drips humidity
It is light but the sun forgot to rise
Don't breathe too deeply
Or you will drown

Carl 26Oct11

The River is Dropping

Typhoon rain and wind
Rushed up the Mekong valley
Raising the water level thirty feet
Backing up into Tong le Sap
Tripling its size

Six weeks later the river was falling
The farmers were following the river down
Fishing in the water
Planting the silt covered banks
With pole beans, bananas,and taro

Time flows onwards.
carl30Oct11

The Killing Field

An overcast morning
At the end of the monsoon season.
I visited the reborn Phnom Penh,
The City of Ghosts.
I stopped at the Russian market
For a wide-brimmed hat
Anticipating a short trip to Choeung Ek
To see the Killing Field.

15km south
Through thinning businesses and homes
Behind the houses ran the river
Where rice and morningglory were raised

Passing through Choeung Ek
We found the glass-faced memorial stupa
Filled with unidentified skulls
Of 8000 victims executed
And buried in the Killing Fields

Under a gloomy sky we walked among the burial pits
Grown over with green turf and trees
Looking like a tough golf course
Pits containing remains of
Men bludgeoned to death to save bullets
Women unclothed
Children smashed against the killing tree
Pits containing rags and bones and teeth of the victims

Remains of 8985 people have been exhumed
Many were brought alive from Tuol Sleng,
The secret service headquarters,
Up to 300 a day for killing

Under grey sky and a weak sun
This is a monument to cruelty and insanity
And the indifference of the outside world
A memorial to gentle poor people who did not resist
A lesson to future generations
Who think selfishly only of themselves
Who ignore corruption, tyranny and repression
Who do not participate in government
Carl2Nov11

Tuol Sleng (S-21)

In the outskirts of the City of Ghosts
Sat the Tuol Svay Prey High School
When Phnom Pehn's people
Were ordered to leave town
And sent to the countryside
To meet Pol Pot's dream f
"Return to the old agrarian ways"
The school was desecreated,
Degraded, and modified
To serve as a Khmer Rouge interrogation and torture center.

Tuol Sleng, secret department S-21
1975 to 1979
Run by Comrade Duch
14,000 men, women and children were "processed"-
Tortured and the majority killed
Grisley place.

Carl2Nov11

Ox Carts

Out in rural Cambodia and Vietnam
The Ford F-150 and Toyota Tundra
Are replaced by the ox cart

Off to the market
Out in the fields
Decked out for holidays
Jouncing along trails
And unimproved roads
Carl2Nov11

Rubber Trees

A rubber tree produces latex sap
The water is removed leaving
Raw rubber.

Ford and Edison had rubber plantations
In Brazil, Malaysia, and Vietnam.
Japan's coveting Malaysian rubber
Started WWII.
The US wanting Vietnamese rubber
Caused another war.

Most rubber is plantation raised
Young plants produced from cuttings or seeds
Are planted in rows and tended

At seven year trees are slashed for 30 years
A spout leads the latex to a collection bowl
A plastic ribbon is tied above the slash
To divert water from the bowl
The latex is boiled or roasted